The Property Risk Playbook (Standard Edition)

Negotiation Tools, Proven Templates, & Closing Tactics for Confident Homebuyers

Damian Martinez

Amado Media Group

Amado Media Group

Standard Edition – First Edition - December 2025

Published by Damian Martinez

For important legal disclaimers and limitations of liability, see the Legal Disclaimer section of this book.

HomeDataReports.com

Printed in the United States of America

Book Dedication

Dedicated to keeping the American Dream exactly that—a dream, not a nightmare. May you close with your eyes wide open, your leverage intact, and your confidence unshaken.

Legal Disclaimer

Please Read Carefully Before Using This Book

No Professional Relationship Established

The information in this book is provided for educational and informational purposes only. By reading this book, you acknowledge and agree that:

The author is NOT:

A licensed real estate agent or broker

A licensed attorney or legal professional

A licensed insurance agent or broker

A certified financial advisor, planner, or mortgage professional

A licensed home inspector or property evaluator

A licensed contractor, engineer, or construction professional

A licensed appraiser or real estate valuation expert

A tax professional or certified public accountant

Nothing in this book creates an attorney-client relationship, real estate representation agreement, insurance advisory relationship, financial advisory relationship, or any other professional service relationship between you and the author.

Educational Purpose and Industry Context

This book is designed to educate prospective homebuyers about negotiation strategies, inspection contingencies, seller concessions, contract terms, and transaction execution. The content integrates property risk intelligence as a foundation for strategic negotiation.

Important Market Context:

The property risk intelligence industry is rapidly evolving. As of December 2025, major real estate portals have faced pressure from industry stakeholders regarding the display of comprehensive risk data. Some platforms have removed or limited climate risk disclosures following concerns from real estate professionals about impact on transaction velocity. This book advocates for informed decision-making based on comprehensive data, recognizing that transparency may conflict with traditional industry practices that prioritize transaction speed over buyer education.

The content is intended to help readers:

Understand negotiation leverage points using documented property intelligence

Learn how to evaluate inspection findings and contractor bids strategically

Make informed decisions about price reductions versus repair credits based on long-term financial analysis

Execute inspection contingencies systematically while protecting earnest money deposits

Use property risk data (flood zones, environmental concerns, climate projections, etc.) as negotiation leverage

Understand the broader market context affecting property transactions, including insurance market dynamics

This book is NOT intended to:

Provide legal advice about contracts, disclosures, or real estate law

Replace professional guidance from licensed real estate agents, attorneys, or inspectors

Guarantee specific negotiation outcomes or financial results

Serve as a substitute for professional contract review or legal counsel

Offer tax, accounting, or financial planning advice

Create binding agreements or legal obligations

Discourage property purchases based on documented risks

Replace professional home inspections or specialized assessments

Property Risk Data: Sources, Limitations, and Probabilistic Nature

This book references property risk intelligence derived from federal databases including but not limited to FEMA flood maps, NOAA climate projections, USGS seismic hazard assessments, EPA environmental databases, U.S. Census demographic data, and other authoritative government sources.

Critical Understanding of Risk Data:

Probabilistic, Not Deterministic: Property risk assessments based on climate modeling, seismic projections, flood probability, and environmental exposure are inherently probabilistic. They represent statistical likelihood based on historical patterns and forward-looking projections, not guarantees of future events. A property designated as "low risk" can still experience disasters. A property designated as "high risk" may never experience the projected event during your ownership.

Data Aggregation Methodology: Property intelligence platforms (including those operated by the author) aggregate data from multiple federal sources using proprietary methodologies. Different platforms may produce different risk assessments for the same property based on:

Weighting algorithms applied to different risk factors

Inclusion or exclusion of specific data sources

Timeframes and recency of underlying data

Geographic resolution and boundary definitions

Assumptions embedded in predictive modeling

Industry Controversy: As documented in December 2024, major property platforms faced criticism from real estate industry stakeholders who disputed the accuracy and interpretation of aggregated risk scores. Some industry groups have characterized certain risk designations as "arbitrary," "inaccurate," or "stigmatizing" to properties. The author believes consumers deserve access to comprehensive risk intelligence, while acknowledging legitimate debates about methodology, accuracy, and interpretation exist within the industry.

No Guarantee of Accuracy: While federal data sources are authoritative, they are:

Updated on varying schedules (FEMA maps update on rolling cycles, USGS seismic models update approximately every 6 years, EPA databases update continuously)

Subject to revision based on new scientific understanding

Limited by historical data availability and quality

Potentially outdated for specific properties

Subject to human and technical errors in collection, processing, and distribution

Independent Verification Required: You must independently verify all property risk data with:

Current federal databases (FEMA.gov, NOAA.gov, USGS.gov, EPA.gov)

Licensed insurance agents for coverage availability and premium costs

Local government agencies for zoning, permits, and code compliance

Professional inspectors and engineers for property-specific assessments

Real estate attorneys for legal implications of disclosed risks

Insurance Market Dynamics and Limitations

The Property Insurance Crisis Context:

As of December 2025, significant disruption exists in U.S. property insurance markets, particularly in high-risk regions. Major carriers have reduced coverage availability, exited certain markets entirely, or substantially increased premiums in areas facing elevated climate, wildfire, flood, or catastrophic risk exposure. Some properties have become effectively "uninsurable" through standard market channels, requiring coverage through state-backed insurers of last resort (FAIR Plans) at significantly higher premiums.

Critical Disclaimers:

This book does NOT:

Provide insurance advice, underwriting guidance, or coverage recommendations

Guarantee property insurability based on risk data or assessments

Predict future insurance costs, carrier availability, or market conditions

Replace consultation with licensed insurance agents or brokers

Guarantee that properties with documented risks can obtain affordable coverage

You MUST:

Obtain insurance quotes from multiple licensed carriers BEFORE making offers

Verify coverage availability for specific property addresses, not general areas

Understand that risk data shown in property intelligence reports does NOT determine insurability—carriers use proprietary underwriting models that may differ substantially from publicly available risk assessments

Recognize that insurance markets can change rapidly—coverage available today may be unavailable or unaffordable at renewal

Consult licensed insurance professionals about coverage requirements, costs, and long-term availability

Insurance Crisis as Negotiation Context: While this book discusses using insurance cost implications as negotiation leverage, the author makes no guarantee that:

Sellers will accept insurance-related repair requests or price reductions

Properties with elevated insurance costs are necessarily "bad investments"

Future insurance markets will improve or deteriorate

Regulatory changes will or will not affect availability or pricing

Professional Consultation Absolutely Required

Real estate transactions involve complex legal, financial, and contractual obligations that vary significantly by jurisdiction. **Before making any offer, signing any contract, or making any binding commitment, you MUST consult with licensed professionals.**

Required professional consultations include:

Real Estate Attorney (CRITICAL—Non-Negotiable):

Contract review and negotiation guidance specific to your state and jurisdiction

Disclosure requirement interpretation and compliance verification

Contingency clause evaluation and exercise procedures

Title examination and ownership verification

State-specific legal protections and buyer rights

Dispute resolution strategies if negotiations break down

Enforcement of contract terms and remedies for breach

Licensed Real Estate Agent or Broker:

Professional negotiation representation and advocacy

Market analysis and comparable sales data

Contract preparation, submission, and amendment coordination

Communication with sellers, seller agents, inspectors, and other transaction parties

Local market customs, standard practices, and regional norms

Transaction timeline management and deadline tracking

Access to Multiple Listing Service (MLS) and professional networks

Licensed Home Inspector:

Comprehensive property condition evaluation meeting state standards

Major system assessment (roof, HVAC, electrical, plumbing, foundation, structural)

Safety hazard identification and documentation

Repair cost estimates and priority recommendations

Specialist referrals when issues exceed general inspection scope (structural engineers, environmental assessors, etc.)

Written inspection reports suitable for negotiation documentation

Licensed Contractors and Specialists:

Written repair estimates for negotiation documentation meeting local standards

Specialist inspections (foundation, electrical, mold, termite, septic, well, radon, environmental)

Scope of work verification and cost accuracy

Permit and code compliance assessment

Contractor licensing and insurance verification

Mortgage Professional or Lender:

Seller concession limit verification for your specific loan type and down payment amount

Appraisal requirement clarification and coordination

Loan-to-value ratio impacts from price reductions versus repair credits

Closing cost structure and cash-to-close calculations

Underwriting guideline interpretation and compliance

Pre-approval accuracy and funding timeline management

Licensed Insurance Agent or Broker:

Homeowners insurance quotes and coverage verification for specific properties

Flood insurance requirements, costs, and coverage limits

Hazard-specific coverage needs (earthquake, wind, fire, hurricane)

Claims history review and implications

Coverage availability assessment in high-risk areas

Carrier financial strength ratings and long-term viability

Tax Professional or CPA:

Property tax implications of purchase price versus assessed value

Deductibility of repairs versus improvements for investment properties

Capital gains considerations and tax planning

State and local tax variation impacts

Long-term tax strategy related to property ownership

The author cannot and does not provide any of these professional services. Attempting to negotiate a real estate transaction without appropriate licensed professionals significantly increases your risk of legal disputes, financial loss, missed deadlines, forfeited earnest money, and unfavorable contractual outcomes.

No Guarantee of Negotiation Results or Outcomes

Following the strategies, frameworks, and guidance in this book does **not** guarantee:

That sellers will accept your repair requests or price reduction proposals

That you will successfully negotiate favorable concessions or contract terms

That inspection contingencies will be included in your contract or honored by sellers

That you will receive credits at closing as requested

That appraisals will support your requested price changes or negotiated values

That lenders will approve your proposed concession structures or financing

That contractors will provide estimates within your timeline or budget

That you will save money compared to accepting properties as-is

That negotiation strategies effective in one market will work in another

That timing and documentation alone guarantee seller cooperation

Any specific financial, legal, contractual, or negotiation outcome

Real estate negotiations involve countless variables beyond the scope of this book, including but not limited to:

Seller motivation, financial position, and emotional attachment to property

Market conditions (buyer's market versus seller's market dynamics)

Property condition, repair complexity, and contractor availability

Competing offers and buyer competition intensity

Agent skill, experience, negotiation style, and commission incentives

Lender requirements, underwriting standards, and appraisal guidelines

Appraisal results, comparable sales selection, and valuation methodology

Contract language, contingency clauses, and legal interpretation specific to your jurisdiction

Timing pressures, deadline management, and scheduling coordination

Seller's agent's advice, influence, and negotiation strategy

Inspection findings, specialist assessments, and repair cost estimates

Local customs, standard practices, and regional market norms

Economic conditions, interest rates, and financing availability

Your results will vary dramatically based on your specific circumstances, the property you're negotiating for, market conditions at the time, the professionals you hire, seller responses, and many factors outside the author's control, prediction, or influence.

Contract Terms, Legal Requirements, and Jurisdictional Variation

Real estate contracts, disclosure obligations, inspection periods, contingency rights, seller concession limits, and legal procedures vary **significantly** by state, county, municipality, and even by specific contract form used.

Examples of jurisdictional variation:

California: 17-day inspection contingency standard, extensive seller disclosure requirements (Transfer Disclosure Statement, Natural Hazard Disclosure), buyer-friendly contingency language, specific cancellation procedures

Texas: 7-10 day inspection periods common, different disclosure forms (Seller's Disclosure Notice), separate amendment processes, different contingency exercise procedures

Florida: 10-15 day inspection periods typical, hurricane/flood specific disclosure requirements, varying contract forms, different timelines

New York: Attorney review period standard (3 days), fundamentally different contract structures, co-op board approval processes, different closing procedures

Pennsylvania: Different disclosure forms (Seller Property Disclosure Statement), well/septic testing requirements, local transfer tax variation, different contingency language

What's legally required, standard practice, or permissible in one state may be:

Prohibited, uncommon, or unenforceable in another state

Subject to different timelines, notice procedures, or exercise requirements

Governed by different disclosure laws, liability standards, or buyer protections

Executed through different contract forms, amendments, or addenda

Interpreted differently by local courts or real estate commissions

You MUST:

Verify all legal requirements with a licensed attorney in your specific jurisdiction

Use contract forms appropriate to your state, county, and local customs

Understand your state's specific contingency exercise procedures and deadlines

Comply with local disclosure, inspection, and negotiation standards

Research whether your state allows specific negotiation strategies discussed in this book

Understand that some strategies effective in buyer-friendly states may be inappropriate or ineffective in seller-friendly jurisdictions

The author provides general educational frameworks applicable across multiple jurisdictions but cannot account for the thousands of variations in real estate law, contract requirements, disclosure obligations, and local practices across the United States.

Data Currency, Market Changes, and Forward-Looking Limitations

The negotiation strategies, market examples, cost estimates, insurance market conditions, and real estate practices described in this book are current as of the publication date (December 2025).

However:

Real estate markets change rapidly: Buyer's markets become seller's markets. Negotiation leverage shifts. Standard practices evolve. What works in a slow market may fail in competitive conditions. Days on market decrease. Multiple offer scenarios increase. Market dynamics can change within weeks.

Lender requirements change regularly: Seller concession limits, appraisal standards, underwriting guidelines, and loan program rules are revised by Fannie Mae, Freddie Mac, FHA, VA, and private lenders on rolling schedules. Guidelines in effect at publication may differ from guidelines at time of use.

Insurance markets fluctuate dramatically: Carrier availability, premium rates, coverage terms, and underwriting standards change—sometimes within months—based on recent disasters, regulatory changes, reinsurance market conditions, and corporate strategy decisions. Insurance discussed in this book reflects December 2025 market conditions.

Contractor costs vary significantly: Repair estimates, labor rates, material costs, and permit fees change based on economic conditions, supply chain factors, regional demand,

and seasonal variation. Cost examples in this book are illustrative only.

Legal precedents evolve: Court decisions, legislative changes, regulatory updates, and administrative interpretations may alter disclosure requirements, buyer protections, contract interpretation, or negotiation standards after publication.

Federal data sources update continuously: Property risk information from FEMA, EPA, NOAA, USGS, and other sources is updated on varying schedules. Information current at publication may be superseded by updated maps, revised projections, new scientific findings, or corrected data.

Property intelligence platforms evolve: The platforms referenced in this book (including those operated by the author) update methodologies, add data sources, revise algorithms, and improve accuracy over time. Risk assessments generated today may differ from assessments for the same property generated in future months or years.

The author makes no guarantee that any strategy, example, cost estimate, timeline, market condition description, or recommendation remains current, effective, applicable, or accurate at the time you use this book. You are responsible for verifying all information with current sources, licensed professionals, and authoritative databases.

Case Studies, Examples, and Illustrative Scenarios

Negotiation examples, case studies, dollar amounts, timelines, seller responses, and transaction outcomes presented in this book are based on documented real estate transactions, inspection reports, court records, news accounts, and professional experience.

However:

Names, locations, and identifying details are modified, composited, or anonymized to protect privacy

Dollar amounts represent typical ranges observed across multiple markets but vary significantly by location, property type, market conditions, and time period

Outcomes described are not guaranteed to occur in similar situations or with similar fact patterns

Negotiation results depend on countless variables unique to each transaction, many of which are unknowable at the time examples are presented

Your specific situation, property, market, timing, and participants will likely differ materially from any example presented

Seller responses illustrated represent possible outcomes, not predictable or guaranteed responses

Examples are educational illustrations designed to demonstrate concepts and frameworks. They should not be interpreted as predictions, promises, guarantees, templates for verbatim use, or assurances that similar strategies will produce similar results in your transaction.

Inspection Contingencies, Legal Deadlines, and Earnest Money Protection

Multiple chapters in this book discuss inspection contingencies, contingency exercise procedures, deadline management, and earnest money protection strategies.

CRITICAL WARNINGS—READ CAREFULLY:

Missing a contingency deadline—even by hours—can cost you thousands of dollars in forfeited earnest money and eliminate your legal right to walk away from a transaction or renegotiate terms.

Contingency deadlines are:

Legally binding and enforced by contract law in all U.S. jurisdictions

Calculated using specific methodologies (calendar days, business days, or hybrid calculations) that vary by state and contract form

Subject to strict interpretation—courts generally do not excuse late exercise due to misunderstanding, miscommunication, or minor delays

Not extended by verbal agreements—extensions require written amendments signed before original deadline expiration

Forfeited if not exercised properly—late or improper exercise typically results in earnest money forfeiture and binding contract obligation

Late contingency exercise notices may result in:

Forfeiture of earnest money deposit (typically $1,000-$10,000 or 1-3% of purchase price)

Elimination of legal right to cancel contract without penalty

Obligation to proceed with purchase regardless of inspection findings or changed circumstances

Seller's right to pursue specific performance (forcing you to complete purchase)

Potential liability for seller's damages if you breach contract

Verbal communications:

Do NOT satisfy legal notice requirements in most jurisdictions

Do NOT extend deadlines or preserve contingency rights

Do NOT create binding obligations on sellers

Should NEVER be relied upon for contingency exercise, deadline extensions, or contract modifications

Written notice procedures:

Vary significantly by state, county, and contract form

May require specific delivery methods (personal delivery, certified mail, electronic transmission)

May require specific recipients (seller, seller's agent, escrow company)

May require specific formats, language, or reference to contract provisions

Must be delivered (not just sent) before deadline expiration in most jurisdictions

Calendar calculations:

May differ from your assumptions or common understanding

May count or exclude weekends, holidays, or specific dates

May begin on contract acceptance date or day after acceptance

May end at specific times (5pm, midnight, close of business) rather than end of day

Require careful review of contract language and applicable state law

You MUST:

Have a licensed real estate attorney review your contract and explain contingency procedures specific to your jurisdiction before signing

Work with a licensed real estate agent to ensure proper notice timing, format, delivery method, and recipient identification

Understand your state's specific requirements for contingency exercise and deadline calculation

Never rely solely on this book's general guidance for legal deadline compliance or contingency exercise procedures

Track all deadlines using both calendar reminders and professional guidance

Obtain written confirmation of all deadline extensions before original deadlines expire

Deliver all contingency-related notices in writing using approved methods

The author is not responsible if you miss contingency deadlines, forfeit earnest money, fail to properly exercise contract rights, or suffer financial loss due to deadline-related errors. These are legal obligations that require professional guidance specific to your jurisdiction, contract form, and transaction circumstances.

Price Reduction vs. Repair Credit Financial Calculations

Chapters discussing price reductions versus repair credits provide frameworks for analyzing long-term financial implications based on interest rates, loan terms, tax treatment, refinancing scenarios, and ownership timelines.

Important limitations and disclaimers:

Interest rates:

Change constantly based on Federal Reserve policy, bond markets, and economic conditions

May differ significantly from examples shown in this book

Vary by borrower credit profile, loan type, down payment amount, and lender

Cannot be predicted with accuracy for future transactions

Tax treatment:

Varies by individual circumstances including income, filing status, and itemization decisions

Changes with tax law revisions at federal, state, and local levels

Differs for primary residences versus investment properties

Requires analysis by qualified tax professionals, not general frameworks in books

Loan terms and underwriting:

Vary by lender, loan program, down payment amount, and credit profile

Subject to change based on market conditions and regulatory requirements

Include nuances not captured in simplified examples (PMI calculations, escrow requirements, etc.)

Seller concession limits:

Depend on specific loan type, down payment percentage, and occupancy status

Change periodically based on Fannie Mae, Freddie Mac, FHA, VA, and USDA guidelines

May be further restricted by individual lender overlays

Require verification with your specific lender for your specific transaction

Appraisal values:

May not support requested price reductions regardless of negotiation success

Depend on comparable sales selection, appraiser judgment, and market conditions

Cannot be guaranteed or predicted with certainty

May require renegotiation if values come in lower than anticipated

Long-term calculations:

Assume numerous variables that may not match your specific situation

Simplify complex financial interactions for educational purposes

Do not account for transaction costs, opportunity costs, or alternative investment returns

Should not be used as sole basis for financial decisions without professional verification

You MUST:

Verify all financial calculations with your mortgage professional or lender before making decisions

Consult a tax professional about tax implications specific to your individual circumstances

Confirm seller concession limits for your exact loan program, down payment amount, and occupancy type

Understand that break-even calculations are estimates based on assumptions that may not hold

Work with licensed financial advisors for complex scenarios or large financial decisions

The author is not responsible for financial decisions based on general calculation frameworks presented without professional verification, individual analysis, or updated market conditions.

Limitation of Liability

To the maximum extent permitted by law, the author, publisher, HomeDataReports.com, PropertyRiskReports.com, and any affiliated companies, websites, or platforms **disclaim all liability** for any loss, damage, injury, or adverse outcome arising from:

Use or misuse of negotiation strategies, frameworks, or tactics described in this book

Reliance on examples, timelines, cost estimates, or outcomes without professional verification

Decisions made based on this book's content without appropriate legal, financial, or professional counsel

Failure to consult licensed professionals for legal, financial, contractual, or real estate advice

Missed contingency deadlines, improperly exercised contract rights, or forfeited earnest money

Negotiation outcomes that differ from examples, expectations, or predictions

Changes in real estate markets, lender requirements, insurance availability, or legal standards

Variations in state, local, or jurisdictional laws, practices, and contract requirements

Contract disputes, legal claims, earnest money forfeiture, or specific performance actions

Property risk data inaccuracies, updates, revisions, or interpretation differences

Insurance market changes, coverage denials, premium increases, or carrier withdrawals

Appraisal results, valuation disputes, or financing challenges

Seller refusals, counteroffers, or negotiation breakdowns

Professional service provider errors, omissions, or malpractice

Any errors, omissions, inaccuracies, or outdated information in the book's content

You assume all risk associated with using the information in this book for real estate transactions, negotiations, contract execution, and property purchases. The author is not responsible for your negotiation decisions, contract compliance, deadline management, transaction outcomes, or financial results.

Property Risk Intelligence Platform Disclaimers

This book references property intelligence platforms operated by the author, including HomeDataReports.com and PropertyRiskReports.com, which aggregate federal data from multiple sources into comprehensive property reports.

Important clarifications:

Platform Independence:

Property intelligence platforms operated by the author are separate businesses from this book

Using the book does not require purchasing platform services

Platform services are optional resources, not mandatory for implementing book strategies

Platform Terms of Service, Privacy Policy, and specific disclaimers govern platform use separately from this book

Data Aggregation and Methodology:

Platforms aggregate data from FEMA, NOAA, USGS, EPA, Census, and other federal sources using proprietary methodologies

Aggregation, weighting, scoring, and presentation methodologies are subject to change

Different methodologies may produce different risk assessments for identical properties

No guarantee that platform assessments will match assessments from other providers, insurers, or government agencies

No Endorsement or Guarantee:

The author's operation of property intelligence platforms does not constitute endorsement of specific properties, locations, or investment decisions

Platform risk scores are educational tools, not deterministic predictions or guarantees

Consumers must verify all data independently and consult licensed professionals

Platform services do NOT replace professional inspections, insurance quotes, legal advice, or due diligence

Acknowledgment and Agreement

By continuing to read and use this book, you acknowledge that you have read, understood, and agree to this disclaimer in its entirety. You further acknowledge that:

You will retain a licensed real estate attorney to review contracts and provide legal guidance specific to your jurisdiction

You will work with licensed real estate professionals during your transaction

You will verify all property risk data, insurance costs, and market information with licensed professionals and authoritative sources before making decisions

You understand that negotiation results vary and are not guaranteed by strategies or frameworks in this book

You accept full responsibility for contract deadlines, legal requirements, contingency exercise, and transaction outcomes

You will not rely solely on this book for legal, financial, insurance, or professional real estate advice

You understand that laws, markets, insurance availability, and standards change over time

You recognize that property risk data is probabilistic and requires independent verification

You understand the insurance market crisis context and will verify coverage availability independently

You will not hold the author liable for outcomes, changes in market conditions, or professional service provider performance

AI-Assisted Content Development

This book was developed using AI writing tools to accelerate content creation and improve clarity. The author designed all analytical frameworks, chapter structures, data methodologies, and strategic guidance. AI tools assisted with drafting, organization, and explanation of complex concepts, but did not originate the core strategies, provide professional opinions, or make recommendations about specific properties or transactions.

All content was reviewed, edited, fact-checked, and approved by the author. The perspectives, risk assessment frameworks, and strategic recommendations reflect the author's judgment and interpretation of federal data sources and market research.

This disclosure does not alter the terms of this legal disclaimer. The book remains educational content only, not professional advice, and all liability limitations stated above continue to apply in full.

Questions, Concerns, or Professional Guidance

For real estate negotiation guidance, contract review, property risk verification, insurance quotes, or transaction-specific questions, please consult licensed professionals in your jurisdiction.

For comprehensive property intelligence reports aggregating federal data sources, visit **HomeDataReports.com** or **PropertyRiskReports.com**. Platform use is governed by separate Terms of Service and Privacy Policy.

By proceeding past this disclaimer, you accept these terms and agree to use this book solely for educational purposes while seeking appropriate professional guidance for all contract, legal, financial, insurance, and real estate negotiation decisions.

Publication Date: December 2025

Author: Damian Martinez

Website: HomeDataReports.com | PropertyRiskReports.com

This disclaimer applies to both the Standard Edition and Expanded Edition of this book.

IMPORTANT INDUSTRY CONTEXT DISCLOSURE:

As of December 2025, the property risk intelligence industry faces ongoing debate about accuracy, methodology, and appropriate use of aggregated risk data. Major real estate portals have experienced pressure from industry stakeholders regarding transparency and risk disclosure. The author believes consumers benefit from comprehensive risk intelligence while acknowledging that reasonable professionals disagree about optimal disclosure practices, risk assessment methodologies, and the appropriate balance between transparency and transaction efficiency. This book represents the author's perspective advocating for informed consumer decision-making based on comprehensive data access.

Introduction

Welcome friend! I'm genuinely glad you picked up this book to step-up your negotiation game!

Here's why: most homebuyers walk into negotiations with all the wrong leverage.

They fall in love with a house during the showing. They make an emotional offer that same weekend. They waive inspection contingencies because their agent mentions "other buyers are writing cleaner offers." They discover major issues during the inspection but have no idea how to turn findings into negotiation power. They accept whatever the seller offers because they don't know what's reasonable or how to push back professionally.

And they close on a property having left thousands—sometimes tens of thousands—of dollars on the table. Not because they're bad negotiators, but because **no one ever taught them how real estate negotiation actually works.**

This book fixes that problem.

The Knowledge Gap Nobody Talks About:

Here's the uncomfortable truth about homebuying: **information without execution is just trivia.**

You can spend weeks researching FEMA flood maps, EPA environmental data, NOAA climate projections, and USGS seismic hazards. You can pull every federal database. You can understand exactly what risks a property carries.

And then you'll walk into contract negotiations completely unprepared to use that information strategically.

Why? Because understanding property risk and **negotiating based on property risk** are two entirely different skill sets. Most buyers master neither. The rare buyers who figure out the first part still stumble on the second.

I've watched it happen hundreds of times.

Smart buyers who researched flood zones and got insurance quotes—but made offers without inspection contingencies because they didn't realize that's how you protect yourself if the inspection reveals deal-breaking issues.

Educated buyers who hired great inspectors and got detailed reports—but had no idea how to convert inspection findings into documented repair requests with contractor bids attached.

Data-driven buyers who understood compound risks—but couldn't articulate why a $15,000 price reduction beats a $15,000 repair credit for their specific loan type and ownership timeline.

Knowing what to ask for means nothing if you don't know how to ask, when to ask, or how to make the seller actually say yes.

That's what this book teaches. Not theory. Execution.

Why I'm Qualified to Teach This:

Between 2017 and 2019, I worked as a licensed real estate agent. During those two years, I saw every negotiation mistake buyers make—not because they were careless, but because the system is designed to rush them through decisions without proper guidance.

I watched buyers waive inspection contingencies in competitive markets and discover $30,000 in foundation issues after closing with zero recourse.

I watched sellers refuse reasonable repair requests, and I watched buyers cave immediately instead of using their contingency deadline to create pressure.

I watched agents (on both sides of the table) push clients toward closing deals regardless of whether the terms protected the buyer, because that's how agents get paid.

I left the industry in 2019, frustrated by how broken the process was.

But I didn't stop helping people buy homes. In 2020, I bought my own house—but I did it differently.

I didn't just pull flood maps and environmental data. I used that data to negotiate. I got contractor bids before submitting my repair request. I structured my inspection timeline to maximize deadline pressure on the seller. I calculated exactly how much a $12,000 price reduction would save me over 30 years versus a $12,000 repair credit, and I negotiated for the option that made financial sense.

I got everything in writing. I exercised my contingency rights when sellers tested my resolve. And I closed with complete clarity about what I was buying, what I'd negotiated, and what I'd saved.

Then friends started asking for help. Not just with property research—but with negotiation strategy.

"The inspection found $18,000 in repairs. What do I ask for? How do I ask? What if they say no?"

"The seller offered a $5,000 credit but the roof needs $14,000 of work. Do I walk away or keep negotiating?"

"Should I take a price reduction or a repair credit? What's the difference long-term?"

I walked them through it. Step by step. Day by day during their inspection periods. How to time contractor bids. How to format repair requests. When to compromise and when to call the bluff. How to protect their earnest money if negotiations broke down.

It worked. They negotiated better concessions. They walked away from bad deals before losing money. They closed on properties with terms that actually protected them.

After helping dozens of people individually, I realized I needed to scale this knowledge.

So I built **HomeDataReports.com**—a platform that aggregates federal property risk data into comprehensive reports for any U.S. address. Today we're working toward helping tens of thousands of property buyers monthly across the country through HomeDataReports and our affiliated websites.

But reports only solve half the problem. **Buyers also need to know what to do with the information.**

That's why I wrote this book. To teach you the execution side. The negotiation frameworks. The contingency strategies. The exact process for turning inspection findings into documented leverage.

<u>What This Book Will Teach You:</u>

This book assumes you've done your homework on property risk. Maybe you read the first book in this series. Maybe you ran your own federal database research. Maybe you hired professionals to assess risk for you.

Regardless of how you got the knowledge, **this book shows you how to use it.**

Over the next chapters, you'll learn:

Why most buyers negotiate from weakness—and how to flip that dynamic by understanding what sellers actually fear (Chapter 11)

How to build a negotiation strategy based on property condition, market leverage, and documented findings rather than emotional reactions (Chapter 11)

The inspection contingency playbook—how to use deadline pressure, contractor bids, and contingency rights to create real negotiating power without threats or ultimatums (Chapter 13)

Price reduction vs. repair credit analysis—the long-term financial math that determines which structure saves you more money over 5, 10, or 30 years depending on your loan terms and ownership plans (Chapter 14)

When walking away is success—how to recognize bad-faith sellers, protect your earnest money, and exercise contingencies before it's too late

How to document everything—the specific formats, timelines, and communication strategies that turn vague concerns into seller concessions

Some of this might not apply to your specific market or situation. If you're in a seller's market where properties get 10 offers in 48 hours, you'll negotiate differently than in a buyer's market with 90 days on market. If your state gives you 7-day inspection periods instead of 17 days, your timeline strategy adjusts.

But the frameworks work everywhere. The principles are universal. And even if a specific tactic doesn't fit your current purchase, it might help a friend buying in another state, or prepare you for your next transaction, or give you insight into how the other side thinks.

Real estate negotiation is a skill that compounds over time. The more you understand, the better you negotiate—not just on this purchase, but on future refinancing, selling, investment properties, and helping family members avoid expensive mistakes.

How This Book Is Different:

I'm not going to give you scripts to memorize or templates to copy-paste. Real estate negotiation doesn't work that way. Every property is different. Every seller has different motivations. Every market has different dynamics.

What I **will** give you is the strategic framework—the underlying logic of how negotiation leverage actually works. How to think about timing, documentation, and pressure. How to make professional requests that sellers take seriously. How to protect yourself when deals go sideways.

You'll see real examples with real numbers. You'll learn what works and what doesn't. You'll understand why certain strategies create leverage and others just annoy everyone involved.

And you'll be able to adapt these frameworks to your specific situation with confidence.

A Word of Warning:

This book will make you a more effective negotiator. That's the goal. But **negotiation effectiveness and legal compliance are not the same thing.**

Real estate contracts involve legally binding deadlines, state-specific contingency procedures, disclosure requirements that vary by jurisdiction, and complex financial structures that interact with loan underwriting rules.

You absolutely, positively must work with licensed professionals:

A real estate attorney to review your contract and explain your legal rights.

A real estate agent to represent you and execute the technical side of negotiations.

A home inspector to document property condition professionally.

Licensed contractors to provide written repair estimates.

A mortgage professional to verify seller concession limits and appraisal requirements.

This book teaches you the strategy. The professionals execute the tactics within your state's legal framework.

Do not attempt to negotiate a real estate transaction alone using only this book. That's not what it's for. It's for making sure you understand the game before the professionals play it on your behalf.

Let's Get To Work:

By the time you finish this book, you'll understand real estate negotiation better than 95% of homebuyers.

You'll know how to time repair requests for maximum pressure. You'll know when to push and when to walk. You'll know exactly how much a price reduction saves you versus a repair credit based on your specific loan terms. You'll know how to protect your earnest money if the seller plays games.

And most importantly, you'll negotiate from strength instead of fear.

That's the difference between leaving money on the table and getting terms that actually protect your investment.

Let's make sure you're in the second group.

— **Damian Martinez**

Founder, HomeDataReports.com

P.S. — If you haven't done your property risk research yet, you might want to start with the first book in this series or run a comprehensive property intelligence report at HomeDataReports.com. Negotiation strategy works best when built on solid data. But if you've already got the knowledge and just need to learn how to use it, you're in exactly the right place.

Contents

Chapter 1

From Knowledge to Action

You're here because you're in motion. Maybe you're already touring homes. Maybe you're comparing neighborhoods, running numbers, or preparing to negotiate. Wherever you are in the process, this book meets you at the moment when information becomes leverage—the exact point where smart buyers separate themselves from everyone else.

Consider a real scenario many buyers find themselves in.

Alex and Jordan discovered a $425,000 home that felt like the one. Great layout, great street, great location. The only small concern was a line buried in the listing: "Located in a moderate flood zone." Nothing dramatic. Nothing alarming. Just a detail most buyers would overlook.

Instead of guessing, they checked. A quick insurance quote told the full story. Flood-zone cost: **$3,200/year**. Comparable non-flood home: **$1,200/year**.

That extra $2,000 per year is easy to ignore in the excitement of house hunting—until you multiply it over a 30-year mortgage. That's roughly **$60,000** in additional lifetime cost.

Most buyers either walk away too quickly or proceed without adjusting their offer. Alex and Jordan did neither. They gathered the FEMA map, documented the insurance quotes, calculated the 30-year cost difference, and presented the numbers professionally.

The seller's first reaction was familiar: "It's never flooded." But data is persuasive. Seeing the long-term financial impact in black and white, the seller agreed to a **$28,000 price reduction**.

Alex and Jordan didn't avoid risk. They didn't get lucky. They simply acted on information.

Knowledge without action leads to the same outcome as not knowing at all.

This book teaches you how to turn property intelligence into negotiation power, cost savings, and long-term confidence. Let's begin with why most buyers never use the data available to them—and how you won't make that mistake.

Why Most Buyers Fail to Negotiate with Data

Here's the uncomfortable truth: every buyer has access to property risk information. FEMA flood maps are public. Wildfire risk zones are documented. Earthquake probabilities are published. Insurance quotes are free. Yet most buyers close on properties paying full price—then discover the risks later when the bills arrive.

Why does this keep happening?

Fear of appearing difficult. Many buyers worry that asking tough questions or requesting price adjustments will offend the seller or kill the deal. They convince themselves that good buyers accept the property "as-is" and move forward gracefully.

Assuming the seller knows best. When sellers say "We've never had a problem," buyers often take that at face value. They don't realize that the seller's 8-year experience doesn't predict the next 30 years—or that the seller has strong financial motivation to minimize concerns.

Trusting the agent to handle everything. Real estate agents are valuable professionals, but they're not your personal investigator. Unless you specifically ask them to dig into property risks and present negotiation strategies, they'll focus on getting the deal closed. That's their job.

Believing negotiation is confrontational. Buyers imagine tense conversations, damaged relationships, and awkward standoffs. In reality, data-driven negotiation is professional problem-solving. You're not accusing anyone of wrongdoing. You're addressing documented financial realities.

Not knowing what's possible. Most buyers simply don't realize that price adjustments based on property risks are common, expected, and entirely reasonable. They think the asking price is the real price.

> □ **RED FLAG #1:** If your agent discourages you from researching property risks or suggests that sellers "won't negotiate," find a different agent.

The result? Buyers pay full price for homes with flood insurance that costs double the national average. They absorb wildfire mitigation costs that should have been split with the seller. They cover foundation repairs that an inspection revealed before closing.

This isn't about being aggressive. It's about being informed and fair.

How Data-Driven Negotiation Works

Here's what changes when you negotiate with data instead of emotion:

Sellers expect negotiation. They've already factored it into their pricing strategy. When you present documented costs tied to property risks, you're playing the game exactly as they anticipated. The only difference is that you're doing it well.

Numbers remove emotion. When you say "I'm concerned about flood risk," the seller hears opinion. When you say "Flood insurance will cost me $3,200 annually instead of the typical $1,200, which equals $60,000 over 30 years," the seller hears facts.

Documentation creates credibility. A casual mention of "potential problems" gets dismissed. A printed insurance quote, a FEMA map, and a cost breakdown from a licensed contractor gets taken seriously.

You gain leverage by creating options. Sellers negotiate when they believe you're willing to walk away. Data doesn't just support your position—it gives you the confidence to mean it when you say "This is my offer based on the actual costs."

Professional presentation matters. How you deliver information determines whether the seller sees you as a problem or a serious buyer making a reasonable request. The tone isn't "You're trying to cheat me." It's "Here's the financial reality we both need to address."

□ **ACTION STEP 1:** Before making an offer on any property, run a property risk report and get at least two insurance quotes.

This system works because it aligns with how professional negotiations actually happen. You're not inventing a new approach—you're using the same framework that experienced investors and commercial buyers use every single day.

Warning Signs: When Sellers Resist Data

Not every seller will negotiate fairly, even when presented with clear documentation. Watch for these warning signs:

Refusing to acknowledge documented costs. If you show insurance quotes and the seller insists "That can't be right," they're either uninformed or unwilling to negotiate honestly.

Claiming the buyer "should have known." Sellers who say "The flood zone is public information" are technically correct—but they're also deflecting responsibility for a cost that affects the home's value.

Offering token concessions instead of real adjustments. A seller who counters your $20,000 request with a $2,000 credit isn't negotiating—they're stalling and hoping you'll accept inadequate compensation.

Pressuring you to "just accept it." Any version of "This is the best you'll find" or "Other buyers didn't have a problem with it" is a red flag. Translation: I'm not willing to share the financial burden fairly.

Getting defensive about questions. Professional sellers understand that buyers need to verify information. Defensiveness usually signals either hidden problems or an unwillingness to negotiate at all.

□ **RED FLAG #2:** If a seller refuses to provide documentation that should be readily available (past insurance claims, flood certificates, or prior inspection reports), walk away.

When you encounter these behaviors, you have a clear decision to make: accept the risk at full price, walk away, or find a property where the seller negotiates fairly.

Your Four-Step Approach

Here's exactly how to apply this framework to every property you're considering:

Step 1: Run the numbers before making an offer. Get insurance quotes for the specific property. Compare them to typical costs for similar homes in lower-risk areas. Calculate the difference over 30 years. This is your baseline data.

Step 2: Document everything. Save the insurance quotes. Print the FEMA maps, wildfire risk assessments, or seismic reports. Get written estimates from contractors for any mitigation work. Create a one-page summary with sources clearly cited.

Step 3: Present your case professionally. Share the documentation with your agent and request that it be presented to the seller as part of your offer or counter-offer. Frame it as "Based on documented costs, we're requesting a $X adjustment to reflect the long-term financial impact."

Step 4: Be willing to walk away. This is the most important step. If the seller won't negotiate fairly, you have other options. Your willingness to walk away isn't a bluff—it's the foundation of your negotiating power.

□ **ACTION STEP 2:** Before your next property tour, bookmark three insurance quote comparison sites so you can run quotes within 24 hours of finding a home you like.

The entire process takes less time than most buyers spend choosing paint colors. But the financial impact can reach tens of thousands of dollars.

Understanding Your Risk Tolerance

Not every risk is a dealbreaker. The goal isn't to avoid all risk—it's to know what you're accepting and pay a fair price for it.

Some buyers are perfectly comfortable living in a flood zone if the insurance cost is built into their budget. Others refuse to consider any property with elevated wildfire risk, regardless of price adjustments.

This approach works best if you:

- Value long-term financial planning over short-term emotion
- Believe a fair price should reflect measurable risks
- Can separate feelings from financial decision-making
- Are willing to walk away if negotiations don't reflect reality

This approach might not work if you:

- Are extremely conflict-averse
- Have found "the one" and won't consider other properties
- Prefer to let your agent handle every detail
- Would rather pay more for a simple process
- Cannot walk away under any circumstances

> If you cannot walk away, you cannot negotiate effectively. Your willingness to move on is the foundation of your leverage.

The key is honest self-assessment. If you know you'll accept the property regardless of what you discover, don't waste time negotiating. But if you're genuinely willing to find a better deal elsewhere, this framework gives you the tools to do it.

What Happens When You Negotiate with Data

Consider what happened to a first-time buyer in the Phoenix area. They found a $390,000 home in an excellent school district with beautiful landscaping. After running a property intelligence report, they discovered moderate wildfire risk due to nearby vegetation and local wind patterns. The home, built in 2005, lacked modern fire-resistant upgrades.

Their insurance quote reflected the exposure: **$2,400 per year**, compared to approximately **$1,200 per year** for similar homes in lower-risk zones. Fire mitigation contractors estimated **$12,000** for safety upgrades, including ember-resistant vents, defensible space landscaping, and roof improvements.

Before learning this negotiation system, they would have purchased the home at full price, discovered the insurance increase later, and covered the $12,000 in upgrades out of pocket—absorbing the full burden without realizing there were better options.

After learning how to negotiate with data, everything changed. They used the templates from Chapter 5 to organize insurance quotes, mitigation estimates, and a 30-year cost projection totaling **$48,000**. They requested a **$30,000** price reduction—about 62% of the long-term burden.

The seller countered at **$18,000**. They negotiated to **$24,000**. The buyer used those funds to complete fire mitigation immediately, improving both safety and long-term affordability.

> **THE DIFFERENCE:** $24,000 in savings—earned simply because they knew how to negotiate with data. Total negotiation time: Less than one week.

That's the difference. Not luck. Not aggressive tactics. Just information applied strategically.

Property intelligence without negotiation equals money left on the table.

Moving Forward

You're now convinced that negotiation is worth it. You understand that sellers expect it, that data removes emotion, and that professional presentation creates results.

Next, let's break down the exact 4-step framework you'll use for every property risk. You'll learn how to organize your documentation, calculate your numbers, present your case, and respond when sellers counter your offer.

The templates are built. The scripts are written. You're about to learn exactly what to say, when to say it, and how to walk away if necessary.

Let's move from understanding to execution.

Chapter 1 Key Takeaways

- ◻ Knowledge without action produces the same result as ignorance
  - ◻ Sellers expect negotiation—you're not being difficult by asking
  - ◻ Data removes emotion and creates credibility in negotiations
  - ◻ Professional presentation determines whether sellers take you seriously
  - ◻ Walking away is the foundation of your negotiating power
  - ◻ Risk tolerance varies—understand yours before negotiating
  - ◻ Documented costs can generate savings of $20,000-$30,000+ per transaction

----

Chapter Resources

Feel free to skip ahead if you'd like to continue reading.

Ready to turn knowledge into negotiation power? Create your free account at **HomeDataReports.com** and test our proprietary risk calculator on any U.S. address. Your first Essential property report is free when you sign up—giving you the comprehensive data foundation you need before making any offer. Think of it as the intelligence report for real estate that shows you what's hiding beneath the listing photos. Download our free Chrome extension to research properties instantly while browsing Zillow or Realtor.com.

Share this tool with friends, family, and the professionals in your life—realtors, lenders, insurance agents, and home inspectors can join our partner referral network to provide their clients with professional-grade property intelligence. When you're ready to go deeper, check out the audiobook, digital toolkit, and video masterclass that walk you through real negotiation scenarios step-by-step.

Chapter 2

The Data-Driven Negotiation Framework

Emily and Marcus did not set out to become negotiation experts. They were simply looking for a home that fit their growing family and their budget.

They found it: a $475,000 house on a quiet street, close to work, with the exact layout they wanted. The photos looked great. The neighborhood felt comfortable. The listing mentioned a flood zone and "nearby industrial facilities," but nothing sounded alarming.

Most buyers would have stopped there.

Instead, Emily and Marcus did what you are learning to do in this book—they turned vague concerns into specific numbers.

They pulled insurance quotes and discovered that flood coverage on this home would run about $2,800 more per year than comparable homes outside the flood zone. Over a 30-year mortgage, that single detail translated into roughly $84,000 in additional cost.

They researched the nearby environmental site and found credible estimates showing that if contamination spread, remediation could easily cost $15,000–$30,000 out of pocket.

Then they looked at resale data. Properties near similar environmental hazards were consistently selling 10–15% below comparable homes in cleaner areas. On a $475,000 home, that discount range alone represented $47,500–$71,250 in potential lost value.

When they added it all up, the total financial burden landed between $100,000 and $130,000.

They did not panic. They did not walk away blindly. They built a formula.

Emily and Marcus presented a simple, documented calculation to the seller: a midpoint cost of $115,000 and a request for a $65,000 reduction—roughly 57% of the total. Their message was clear: "We will absorb about half of this long-term risk if you share the other half."

After calls to their own insurance agent and a review of comparable sales, the seller came back at $50,000. They settled together at $55,000 in price reductions and credits.

They saved $55,000 because they had a framework, not just a feeling.

Sellers don't respond to feelings. They respond to evidence, documentation, and math.

This chapter gives you that formula. It's called the **Risk Cost Calculator**, and it's your most powerful negotiation tool.

Why Most Negotiations Fail Before They Start

Most failed negotiations in real estate share the same root problem: the buyer has concerns, but no structure. They see a risk, but cannot articulate its real cost. They know something feels off, but cannot translate that feeling into a credible number.

Sellers do not respond to feelings. They respond to evidence, documentation, and math. That's why most negotiations fall apart before they ever get started.

The Three Common Mistakes

Mistake #1: Arbitrary Requests

Many buyers make their first—and sometimes only—mistake right here.

Buyer: "I want $20,000 off because of the flood risk."

Seller: "Why $20,000?"

Buyer: "Because... it seems fair?"

Seller: "No."

Without documentation, without math, without a clear breakdown of where that number comes from, you have no leverage. The seller sees an emotional reaction, not a business case.

> □ **RED FLAG #1:** If you cannot explain exactly where your number comes from in 60 seconds or less, your seller will dismiss it immediately.

Mistake #2: Vague Concerns

Buyer: "This home is in a flood zone. That's a problem."

Seller: "It hasn't flooded in 30 years."

Buyer: "But it could."

Seller: "Anything could happen."

Now what? You're stuck. You've raised the issue, but you haven't quantified it. The seller can dismiss it with a sentence because you haven't shown them the actual financial impact.

Mistake #3: Emotional Appeals

Buyer: "We're really worried about this environmental site. It makes us nervous."

Seller: "I understand, but the price is firm."

The seller hears: "We're scared, but we have no data." And they move on.

Emotion without documentation gets you nowhere. Documentation without emotion is powerful.

> *The difference between a successful negotiation and a failed one is not how you feel about the risk—it's whether you can prove what that risk actually costs.*

The Risk Cost Calculator: Your Negotiation Formula

The Risk Cost Calculator is a three-part formula that turns any property risk into a specific, defensible number.

> The Risk Cost Calculator Formula: **(Insurance Impact + Mitigation Costs + Resale Impact) × 50–75% = Your Request**

Let's break down each component.

Part A: Insurance Impact

This is the most straightforward piece. What will this risk cost you in additional insurance premiums over the life of your ownership?

How to calculate it:

1. Get actual insurance quotes for the property (not estimates—real quotes)
2. Compare to quotes for similar homes without this risk
3. Calculate the annual difference
4. Multiply by your expected ownership period (typically 7–10 years for most buyers, 30 years if you're calculating full mortgage impact)

Example:

- Insurance with flood risk: $4,200/year
- Insurance without flood risk: $1,800/year

- Annual difference: $2,400
- 10-year ownership period: $24,000
- 30-year mortgage period: $72,000

You now have a real number backed by actual quotes.

□ **ACTION STEP 1:** Get at least 2 insurance quotes for the target property and 2 quotes for comparable homes without the risk factor. Document the difference.

Part B: Mitigation Costs

What will it cost to reduce or eliminate this risk? This includes retrofits, repairs, upgrades, or preventative measures.

How to calculate it:

1. Identify what mitigation is possible (flood barriers, seismic retrofitting, radon mitigation, etc.)
2. Get contractor quotes or use documented industry averages
3. Include both immediate costs and deferred maintenance

Common mitigation cost ranges:

- Flood barriers and drainage improvements: $5,000–$25,000
- Seismic retrofitting (foundation bolting, cripple wall bracing): $8,000–$20,000
- Wildfire defensible space and ember-resistant vents: $3,000–$15,000
- Radon mitigation systems: $1,200–$2,500
- Environmental remediation (soil testing, monitoring): $5,000–$50,000+

Again, use actual quotes whenever possible. Industry averages are fine when quotes aren't practical, but be prepared to show your source.

□ **ACTION STEP 2:** Research mitigation costs for your specific risk. Get contractor estimates or cite documented industry ranges (and save your sources).

Part C: Resale Impact

This is often the largest component—and the one most buyers overlook. What will this disclosed risk cost you when you sell?

Research shows that disclosed risks reduce property values by measurable percentages:

- Wildfire hazard zones: 4–10% discount
- Floodplain designation: 2–16% discount depending on severity
- Earthquake zones (high-risk areas): 3–8% discount
- Environmental contamination sites: 10–20% discount
- Radon-disclosed properties: 2–5% discount

How to calculate it:

1. Research comparable sales of properties with similar disclosed risks
2. Calculate the percentage discount compared to similar homes without that risk
3. Apply that percentage to your purchase price

Example:

- Purchase price: $475,000
- Comparable homes with environmental disclosure: 12% discount on average
- Resale impact: $57,000

This is money you will not recover when you sell—even if the risk never materializes.

> □ **RED FLAG #2:** Resale impact exists even if nothing bad ever happens. Disclosure laws require future sellers to reveal known risks, which means every future buyer will price in that risk just like you should.

Putting It Together

Now you add all three components:

Insurance Impact: $24,000 (10-year ownership) **Mitigation Costs:** $18,000 **Resale**

Impact: $57,000 **Total Calculated Cost:** $99,000

But here's the critical part: **you don't ask for 100% of that cost.**

You ask for **50–75%** of the total calculated cost. This accomplishes three things:

1. **Shows reasonableness.** You're not trying to eliminate all risk—you're asking the seller to share the burden.
2. **Leaves room for negotiation.** Starting at 60% gives you space to settle at 50% if needed.
3. **Demonstrates fairness.** You're explicitly stating you'll absorb part of the cost.

The power of this formula isn't just in the math—it's in showing the seller that you've done your homework and you're being reasonable about splitting the risk.

Using our example:

- Total calculated cost: $99,000
- Your request (60%): $59,400
- Your message: "I'll absorb $40,000 of this risk if you cover $59,000."

Now you have a specific, defensible number backed by documentation and math.

The Four-Step Process: From Data to Dollars

Here's exactly how to apply this framework in your own negotiation:

Step 1: Identify the Risks

Pull your property report from HomeDataReports.com and identify every disclosed risk that carries financial consequences:

- Flood zones
- Wildfire hazard areas
- Seismic activity zones
- Environmental contamination sites

- Radon levels
- Insurance availability issues
- Any other disclosed hazards

Don't skip the small risks. A $3,000 radon mitigation plus a $5,000 resale discount is still $8,000 on the table.

□ **ACTION STEP 3:** List every risk identified in your property report. Rank them by estimated financial impact (highest to lowest).

Step 2: Quantify Each Risk

For each risk you identified, calculate all three components.

Create a simple spreadsheet with these columns:

1. Risk Type
2. Insurance Impact (annual cost × ownership period)
3. Mitigation Costs (quotes or documented ranges)
4. Resale Impact (% discount × purchase price)
5. Total Cost
6. Your Request (50-75% of total)

Example spreadsheet:

Now you have a complete picture of the financial burden—and a specific request backed by documented calculations.

□ **ACTION STEP 4:** Build your Risk Cost Calculator spreadsheet. Include sources for every number (insurance quote screenshots, contractor estimates, comparable sales data).

Step 3: Adjust for Your Risk Tolerance

Not every risk needs to be negotiated. Some risks might be acceptable to you even without a price reduction—especially if they're low-probability or if mitigation is inexpensive.

Ask yourself:

- Is this risk something I'm willing to absorb entirely?
- Would I walk away from this deal if the seller refuses to adjust for this risk?
- Does this risk genuinely affect my long-term costs, or is it mostly theoretical?

If a risk doesn't bother you financially or emotionally, you don't need to negotiate it. Focus your energy on the risks that genuinely impact your decision.

Sarah's Risk Tolerance Decision

Sarah found a $525,000 home in a moderate wildfire zone. Her calculations showed:

- Insurance impact: $18,000 (10 years)
- Mitigation costs: $8,000 (ember vents, defensible space)
- Resale impact: $26,250 (5% discount)
- Total cost: $52,250

She decided the wildfire risk was acceptable given the home's other features, strong fire department response times, and recent vegetation management in the area. She negotiated a $12,000 credit for immediate mitigation work, but didn't push for the full 60% ($31,350).

Result: She focused her negotiating energy on a separate radon issue where she had less tolerance, got the mitigation done upfront, and closed the deal. She still saved $19,000 total across both issues.

The point: **you control which risks you negotiate and how aggressively you push.** The formula gives you the numbers—you decide which numbers matter most.

Step 4: Present Your Case

This is where documentation wins. When you present your request to the seller, you're not making an emotional appeal—you're presenting a business case.

Your presentation should include:

1. **A summary of the risk** (1-2 sentences)
2. **The three-part calculation** (insurance, mitigation, resale)

3. **Your sources** (insurance quotes, contractor estimates, comparable sales)
4. **Your specific request** (50-75% of total)
5. **Your rationale** (explicitly state you're willing to share the burden)

Example presentation:
"Based on the flood zone designation, I've calculated the long-term financial impact:

- Additional flood insurance: $2,400/year × 10 years = $24,000
- Flood mitigation (French drain, sump pump): $12,000 (quote attached)
- Resale discount based on comparable sales: 10% = $47,500 (comps attached)
- Total calculated cost: $83,500

I'm requesting a $50,000 reduction (60% of total). I'll absorb the remaining $33,500 and handle long-term insurance costs. The attached documentation supports each component of this calculation."

Notice what this does:

- It's specific (not "I want a discount for the flood zone")
- It's documented (quotes and comps attached)
- It's reasonable (explicitly sharing the burden)
- It's confident (no apologizing, no hedging)

□ **RED FLAG #3:** If you cannot attach documentation to every number in your request, go back and get it before you present. Sellers will challenge anything that looks like guesswork.

Real-World Examples: The Formula in Action

Let's look at three different buyers who used this exact framework—and saved substantial amounts.

Jake's Seismic Retrofit Negotiation
Property: $920,000 home in California earthquake zone

His Calculation:

- **A: Insurance Impact**
    - Standard earthquake insurance: $4,200/year
    - Most buyers in his area do not carry coverage due to cost
    - 30-year burden: $126,000
- **B: Mitigation Costs**
    - Foundation bolting: $8,000
    - Cripple wall bracing: $6,000
    - Total retrofit: $14,000
- **C: Resale Impact**
    - Retrofitted homes sell 5-8% higher than non-retrofitted
    - On a $920K home: ~$46,000 difference

Total Calculated Cost: $186,000
His Request: $110,000 (59% of total)
His Justification: "I'll absorb long-term insurance costs and some resale risk. You cover the retrofit and a portion of the value impact."

The seller resisted at first: "That's too much."

Jake calmly walked through his spreadsheet. The seller called an earthquake specialist, confirmed the numbers, and came back with a $75,000 offer. They ultimately agreed at **$90,000**.

Jake saved $90K and completed the retrofit using the savings. The difference? **The formula gave him confidence—and credibility.**

Maria's Multi-Risk Strategy
Property: $385,000 home with both radon and minor flood risk
Her Calculation:
RISK #1: Radon (4.8 pCi/L)

- Mitigation system: $2,200
- Resale impact (3%): $11,550

- Subtotal: $13,750

RISK #2: Minor Flood Zone

- Additional insurance: $900/year × 10 years = $9,000
- Resale impact (4%): $15,400
- Subtotal: $24,400

Combined Total: $38,150 **Her Request (65%):** $24,800

The seller initially offered $15,000. Maria showed them comparable sales data proving the resale discounts were real and insurance quotes showing the ongoing costs.

They settled at **$21,000**—and the seller agreed to complete radon mitigation before closing.

Maria's insight: "I had two smaller risks instead of one big one, but the formula worked exactly the same way. The seller couldn't dismiss either risk because I had the numbers."

David's High-Stakes Environmental Negotiation

Property: $695,000 home near a former industrial site with soil contamination

His Calculation:

- **A: Insurance Impact**
  - Environmental liability insurance: $1,800/year × 10 years = $18,000
- **B: Mitigation Costs**
  - Ongoing soil monitoring: $2,500/year × 5 years = $12,500
  - Potential remediation reserve: $25,000
  - Subtotal: $37,500
- **C: Resale Impact**
  - Comparable homes near similar sites: 15-18% discount
  - At 16%: $111,200

Total Calculated Cost: $166,700

His Request (70%): $116,690

The seller was shocked. "That's almost 17% off the asking price!"

David replied: "That's correct. And it reflects a 16% resale discount that I'll face when I sell, plus $55,000 in direct costs I'll absorb. I'm actually asking you to cover only 70% of the total burden. I'll carry 30% myself plus all future liability if contamination worsens."

The seller consulted their own environmental specialist and real estate attorney. After reviewing David's comparables and confirming the resale discount data, they came back at $95,000.

They settled at **$105,000**.

David's takeaway: "The bigger the risk, the more important the documentation becomes. I had 15 pages of comparable sales, environmental reports, and insurance quotes. The seller couldn't argue with the data."

Understanding Risk Tolerance

The Risk Cost Calculator gives you the numbers, but there's one more critical factor: **your personal risk tolerance.**

Two buyers can look at the exact same risk—with the exact same calculated cost—and make completely different decisions.

The formula tells you what the risk costs. Your risk tolerance tells you whether that cost is acceptable.

High Risk Tolerance

Profile: You're comfortable with uncertainty, you have financial reserves, you can handle unexpected costs, or you're experienced with the specific risk type.

Approach: You might negotiate only the most expensive or most certain risks. You might accept smaller risks entirely without negotiation. You might ask for 50% instead of 75%.

Example: A buyer in California who grew up with earthquake risk might not negotiate seismic issues aggressively because they understand the actual probability and have experience managing it.

Moderate Risk Tolerance

Profile: You want to share the burden but you're not trying to eliminate all risk. You can handle some uncertainty if the price reflects it.

Approach: You negotiate the major risks at 50-65% of calculated cost. You might accept minor risks without adjustment if the overall deal is strong.

Example: Emily and Marcus (from the opening story) had moderate tolerance—they were willing to absorb $60,000 of long-term costs if the seller covered $55,000 upfront.

Low Risk Tolerance

Profile: You need certainty, you have limited financial cushion, you cannot afford surprise expenses, or this risk type genuinely concerns you.

Approach: You negotiate more aggressively—asking for 70-75% of calculated costs. You might walk away entirely if the seller won't meaningfully adjust. You prioritize deals where risks are minimal.

Example: A first-time buyer with a tight budget in a flood zone might need the seller to cover most mitigation costs upfront because they cannot afford both the mitigation and a surprise insurance spike in year two.

> Your risk tolerance determines how aggressively you negotiate—but the formula itself never changes. The calculated cost is the same regardless of your tolerance. The difference is in how much of that cost you're willing to absorb.

Why This Formula Wins: The Psychological Advantage

Most buyers think negotiation is about leverage, timing, or persuasion skills. Those matter—but they're secondary.

The real power of the Risk Cost Calculator is psychological.

When you present a documented, formula-based request, you accomplish several things simultaneously:

1. You remove emotion from the negotiation

The seller cannot dismiss your request as "buyer's remorse" or "cold feet" because you're not presenting feelings—you're presenting math.

2. You establish credibility instantly

Most buyers show up with vague concerns. You show up with spreadsheets, quotes, and comparable sales. The seller immediately recognizes they're dealing with someone who's done their homework.

3. You anchor the negotiation around real costs

Once you present a $99,000 calculated cost, that number becomes the anchor. Even if the seller pushes back, they're now negotiating around your documented figure—not their emotional attachment to the listing price.

4. You force the seller to engage with facts

If they want to counter your request, they have to counter your documentation. They can't just say "no"—they have to explain why your insurance quotes, contractor estimates, or comparable sales data are wrong.

Most sellers cannot do that. Because your numbers are real.

When you present documented numbers, the seller has only two options: accept your math or disprove it. And disproving real insurance quotes and actual comparable sales is nearly impossible.

Common Seller Objections—And How to Handle Them

Even with perfect documentation, some sellers will push back. Here's how to respond:

Objection #1: "That's too much."

Your Response: "I understand it feels like a large number. That's because it reflects real, long-term costs I'll be absorbing. I'm actually asking you to cover only [60%] of the calculated total—I'll absorb the other [40%] myself. These aren't made-up numbers; they're based on actual insurance quotes and documented resale data. Would you like to see the documentation?"

Objection #2: "The risk isn't that bad."

Your Response: "That may be your experience, but the market disagrees. Comparable homes with this same disclosure are selling at a [X%] discount. Insurance companies are charging $[X] more per year for this risk. I'm not saying the risk will materialize—I'm saying it carries measurable costs whether it does or not."

Objection #3: "We already priced it in."

Your Response: "If you've already adjusted the price for this risk, then we're aligned on the financial impact. I'd like to understand how you calculated that adjustment so we can compare methodologies. If our numbers are similar, we'll move forward. If they're different, let's discuss why."

(Hint: Most sellers who claim they "priced it in" cannot show you their calculation. This forces them to either admit they didn't actually adjust—or engage with your numbers.)

□ **RED FLAG #4:** If a seller refuses to engage with your documentation entirely—won't look at your quotes, won't review your comps, won't discuss the math—that's a signal they're not negotiating in good faith. Consider whether this is a deal worth pursuing.

Chapter 2 Key Takeaways

□ Most negotiations fail because buyers have concerns but no structure to quantify costs

□ The Risk Cost Calculator formula: **(Insurance Impact + Mitigation Costs + Resale Impact) × 50-75% = Your Request**

□ **Insurance Impact:** Get real quotes, calculate annual difference, multiply by ownership period

□ **Mitigation Costs:** Get contractor estimates or use documented industry ranges

□ **Resale Impact:** Research comparable sales with similar risks, apply percentage discount to your purchase price

□ Always ask for 50-75% of calculated cost (never 100%)—this shows reasonableness and leaves room to negotiate

□ Document everything: insurance quotes, contractor estimates, comparable sales data

□ Your risk tolerance determines how aggressively you negotiate, but the formula never changes

□ Present your case with: risk summary, three-part calculation, sources, specific request, and explicit rationale

□ The formula's power is psychological: it removes emotion, establishes credibility, anchors the negotiation, and forces sellers to engage with facts

□ Use this framework for every risk category in Chapters 4-10—the process is identical regardless of risk type

You now have the most powerful negotiation tool in real estate: a formula that turns any risk into a specific, defensible number backed by documentation and math.

In Chapter 3, you'll get the complete toolkit: ready-to-use templates, scripts, checklists, and decision trees that make this system easy to execute in every real-world scenario.

Chapter Resources
Feel free to skip ahead if you'd like to continue reading.

Your negotiation framework needs a data foundation. Before you can negotiate strategically, you need to know what you're negotiating about. Visit **HomeDataReports.com** to generate comprehensive property intelligence reports that aggregate federal data from FEMA, NOAA, USGS, EPA, and more—the same authoritative sources professionals use. Our risk calculator evaluates properties across multiple categories instantly, giving you the documented risks you'll use during inspection and negotiation. Create your free account today and get your first Essential report at no cost.

Tell your realtor about our partner program—when they join our referral network, they can offer these reports to all their clients and build stronger, more informed relationships. The digital toolkit and video masterclass show you exactly how to use this data during actual negotiations. This is the intelligence advantage that separates strategic buyers from reactive ones.

Chapter 3

Building Your Negotiation Toolkit

Two Buyers, Same Data, Different Outcomes

Buyer #1 and Buyer #2 were looking at the exact same house. Same neighborhood, same inspection report, same Risk Cost Calculator number staring back at them.

Buyer #1 ran the formula, saw a $48,000 long-term risk cost, and decided to "bring it up" with the seller. He fired off a quick text from his phone: "Hey, we found some issues in the report. We'd like $30K off."

No subject line that stood out. No documents attached. No clear breakdown of how he reached $30,000. No follow-up phone call.

The seller's agent read it between showings, shrugged, and replied: "Seller declines." Negotiation over.

Buyer #2 had the same $48,000 number—but treated it like a business case, not a casual request.

Her agent sent a professional email titled: "123 Oak Avenue – Due Diligence Findings and Adjustment Request"

Inside was a simple, organized summary:

- Total calculated long-term risk cost: $48,000
- Specific line items (flood insurance, drainage work, resale impact)
- Three supporting documents attached
- Request for $35,000 price reduction with 72-hour response window

The seller called within 36 hours. They negotiated. Buyer #2 closed with a $28,000 reduction.

Same house. Same data. Different presentation. Different outcome.

Your data means nothing if your presentation screams "I don't know what I'm doing."

The Gap Between Knowing and Doing

Chapter 2 gave you the formula for calculating what to ask for. You can run the numbers. You can identify the risks. You can justify your adjustment request mathematically.

But that's only half the equation.

The other half is tactical execution. How do you present your findings? What communication channel works best? What format convinces a seller you're serious? How do you document everything to protect yourself legally?

Most buyers skip this step. They treat negotiation like a casual conversation instead of a structured business process. They think good data automatically translates to good outcomes.

It doesn't.

> □ **RED FLAG #1:** Sending adjustment requests via text message or casual email kills your credibility instantly. Sellers won't take you seriously if your presentation looks unprofessional.

Professional presentation separates successful negotiations from rejected ones. The seller needs to see that you've done real work, that your numbers are defensible, and that walking away from your offer means losing a serious buyer.

This chapter gives you the tactical tools to make that happen.

The Four-Part Negotiation System

Effective negotiation requires four coordinated elements: templates, communication channels, documentation systems, and professional support. Each serves a specific purpose. Each must be used correctly.

Part 1: Templates (Your Starting Framework)

The templates in Chapters 4-10 aren't copy-paste solutions. They're customizable frameworks that prevent you from forgetting critical details or presenting information poorly.

Each template follows the same structure:

- Clear subject line
- Brief introduction establishing credibility
- Numbered findings with supporting data
- Specific adjustment request with justification
- Reasonable response timeline
- Professional closing

□ **ACTION STEP 1:** Never send a template unmodified. Replace every [BRACKET] with your specific property details, calculations, and documentation.

Bad Template Usage: "Dear Seller, I found [ISSUE] at [PROPERTY ADDRESS] and need [AMOUNT] off the price because [REASON]."

Good Template Usage: "Dear Seller, Following our inspection of 456 Elm Street on November 15, we identified three flood-related concerns requiring remediation. Based on contractor quotes totaling $12,400 and projected insurance increases of $280/month, we're requesting a $22,000 price adjustment. Attached documentation supports each line item."

The difference? Specificity, professionalism, and evidence.

Templates save time and prevent mistakes—but only if you customize them properly. Generic requests get generic rejections.

Part 2: Communication Channels (Choosing the Right Medium)

Not all conversations belong in email. Not all negotiations need face-to-face meetings. Strategic communicators match their medium to their message.

Email: Your Documentation Backbone

Use email when you need a permanent record of what was said and agreed upon. Email creates evidence. It prevents "he said, she said" disputes. It forces both parties to be clear about terms.

Email works best for:

- Initial adjustment requests with supporting documentation
- Listing specific concerns that need written responses
- Following up on verbal conversations to confirm what was discussed
- Establishing deadlines and response windows
- Involving multiple parties (agents, attorneys, inspectors)

Professional email structure matters. Your subject line determines whether the seller's agent opens your message immediately or flags it for "later" (which often means never).

Weak subject lines:

- "Question about the house"
- "Inspection results"
- "Need to talk"

Strong subject lines:

- "Due Diligence Findings – 789 Pine Street"
- "Structural Repair Documentation – Price Adjustment Request"
- "Time-Sensitive: Environmental Data Package"

□ **RED FLAG #2:** Verbal agreements in real estate mean nothing. If it's not documented in writing, it never happened. Always follow phone conversations with summary emails.

Phone: Building Rapport and Handling Objections

Phone calls work best for relationship-building and real-time problem-solving. When you need to explain complex data, respond to seller concerns, or negotiate back-and-forth quickly, pick up the phone.

Use phone calls when:

- You need to establish personal connection before making formal requests
- The seller raised objections to your written proposal and you need to clarify
- Negotiations are stuck and need human conversation to move forward

- You want to gauge tone and sincerity (hard to detect in email)

☐ **ACTION STEP 2:** After every significant phone conversation, send a follow-up email summarizing what was discussed and agreed upon. This creates your documentation trail.

In-Person: When Stakes Are Highest

Face-to-face meetings signal serious commitment. They're time-intensive for both parties, which means they only happen when deals are on the line.

Schedule in-person meetings when:

- Negotiations have reached an impasse and email/phone aren't working
- You're presenting highly technical data that requires visual aids
- The seller is skeptical of your claims and needs to see your evidence firsthand
- Emotional tension is high and you need to reset the relationship

The Communication Sequence:

Most successful negotiations follow this pattern:

1. Phone call to establish relationship and preview findings
2. Email with formal documentation and specific requests
3. Phone follow-up to discuss and negotiate
4. Email confirmation of final agreement
5. In-person meeting only if deal is stuck or stakes justify it

Choose your communication channel strategically. Email creates evidence. Phone builds rapport. In-person resets relationships. Use all three at the right times.

Part 3: Documentation Systems (Building Your Evidence File)

Every negotiation requires proof. You can't just say the property has flood risk—you need to show the FEMA map. You can't claim foundation issues—you need the engineer's report. You can't request pricing adjustments without comparable sales data.

Your Core Documentation Checklist:

- Risk assessment reports (flood maps, environmental data, crime statistics)
- Professional inspection reports (home inspector, structural engineer, specialists)
- Contractor repair quotes (itemized, from licensed professionals)
- Insurance quotes showing elevated premiums
- Comparable sales data from non-affected areas
- Your completed Risk Cost Calculator spreadsheet
- Relevant government maps or regulatory documents

□ **ACTION STEP 3:** Create a single PDF packet containing all supporting documents before sending any adjustment request. Organized evidence = credible buyer.

Documentation Best Practices:

Label everything clearly. "Foundation Report Nov 2025.pdf" is better than "Report.pdf". Organize documents in the order you reference them in your email. Number each attachment so the seller can easily follow your logic.

Store copies of everything. Email threads disappear. Agents forget conversations. Six months after closing, you might need proof of what was agreed upon. Cloud storage is cheap insurance.

□ **RED FLAG #3:** Sending adjustment requests without supporting documentation signals you're guessing. Sellers reject unsupported claims immediately.

Part 4: When to Bring in Professionals

Not every negotiation requires hiring experts. But knowing when professional support justifies its cost can mean the difference between leaving money on the table and securing major adjustments.

When to Hire Professionals:

Real Estate Attorney ($300-$500/hour):

- Complex environmental contamination issues
- Legal disputes over property boundaries or easements
- Seller refuses to negotiate despite documented risks
- Contract modifications beyond standard contingencies
- Title issues discovered during due diligence

Structural Engineer ($400-$800 for inspection):

- Foundation cracks or settlement concerns
- Suspected earthquake or hurricane damage
- Major load-bearing wall modifications
- Roof structural integrity questions
- Insurance company requires engineer certification

Environmental Consultant ($800-$2,000 for Phase I assessment):

- Property near former industrial sites
- Evidence of soil contamination
- Asbestos or lead paint concerns in older homes
- Radon levels above EPA action threshold
- Underground storage tank presence

□ **ACTION STEP 4:** Before hiring any professional, get a written quote and scope of work. Know exactly what you're paying for and what deliverables you'll receive.

The Professional Hiring Decision Tree:

Ask yourself three questions:

1. Is the potential cost savings more than 3x the professional fee?
2. Do I lack the technical expertise to present this issue credibly?

3. Will the seller's insurance or legal team require third-party verification?

If you answer "yes" to any of these, hire the professional.

Professional reports don't just justify your adjustment request—they give sellers legal cover to agree with you.

The Seven Critical Mistakes That Kill Negotiations

Mistake #1: Sending requests without documentation

Saying "I'm worried about flood risk" means nothing. Attaching FEMA maps, insurance quotes, and contractor estimates means everything.

Mistake #2: Making requests before establishing inspection contingencies

Never reveal risk concerns before your inspection period begins. Sellers can withdraw the property or refuse negotiations if you don't have contractual leverage.

Mistake #3: Asking for round numbers

"I want $25,000 off" sounds arbitrary. "I'm requesting $23,750 based on documented costs" sounds calculated and defensible.

Mistake #4: Negotiating emotionally

"This house is falling apart" triggers defensiveness. "Our structural engineer identified three issues requiring remediation" triggers problem-solving.

Mistake #5: Accepting the first counteroffer

Sellers expect negotiation. Their first counteroffer leaves room for movement. Always make at least one counter-counter.

> □ **RED FLAG #4:** If the seller refuses to provide any documentation supporting their position (repair history, previous inspections, permits), walk away. Transparency matters.

Mistake #6: Forgetting to document verbal agreements

Phone conversations and hallway discussions don't count. Every agreement must be confirmed in writing within 24 hours.

Mistake #7: Negotiating without a walk-away number

Before you start, decide your maximum acceptable risk cost. If negotiations don't reach that threshold, you must be willing to terminate.

□ **ACTION STEP 5:** Set your walk-away number before starting negotiations. Write it down. Don't rationalize accepting worse terms later.

Real World Example: The EPA Superfund Case

Marcus found a property near an EPA Superfund site—a location where hazardous waste contamination required federal cleanup. The house wasn't directly contaminated, but proximity mattered for both insurance and resale.

Marcus's Toolkit Approach:

Documentation: Downloaded EPA site assessment reports, documented cleanup timeline, gathered property value studies showing 8-12% discount for homes near Superfund sites.

Communication Strategy: Started with phone call to agent: "I'm very interested in the property, but need to discuss proximity to the EPA site before finalizing my offer."

This preview signaled seriousness without revealing his position.

Formal Request: Sent detailed email with:

- EPA site documentation
- Comparable sales data (non-affected vs. affected properties)
- Risk Cost Calculator showing $42,000 resale impact
- Request for $30,000 adjustment (71% of calculated cost)
- 48-hour response window

Professional Support: Hired environmental consultant ($1,200) to review EPA reports and confirm no direct contamination risk to the property.

Negotiation: Seller countered at $12,000. Marcus provided additional comparable sales data and resale timeline studies. Final agreement: $21,500 reduction.

Result: Marcus secured 71% of his calculated cost ($21,500 of $30,000 requested) and gained documentation showing the property was safe despite proximity to the site.

□ **ACTION STEP 6:** Study successful negotiations in your target market. Join local real estate investor groups to learn what adjustments others have secured and how they structured their requests.

Chapter Recap

Your negotiation toolkit consists of four elements working together:

1. **Templates** provide structure and prevent mistakes—but must be customized with specific data

2. **Communication channels** match medium to message—email for documentation, phone for rapport, in-person for impasse resolution

3. **Documentation systems** provide proof—organized evidence packets demonstrate credibility

4. **Professional support** justifies major requests—know when hiring experts produces ROI

What You've Learned:

- Professional presentation matters as much as the data itself

- Strategic communicators choose email, phone, or in-person based on the situation

- Documentation creates credibility and legal protection

- Professional reports give sellers cover to agree with your requests

- Seven critical mistakes kill negotiations before they start

- Successful buyers know their walk-away number before beginning

Next Steps: Chapter 4 shows you exactly how to negotiate flood costs before closing. You'll get the specific templates, timing, and documentation strategy for one of the most common—and most expensive—property risks buyers face.

Chapter Resources

Feel free to skip ahead if you'd like to continue reading.

Every toolkit needs the right tools. Your negotiation toolkit starts with comprehensive property data you can access in seconds. Install our free Chrome extension from **HomeDa**

taReports.com —it lets you research any property instantly while browsing real estate sites, pulling risk data without opening multiple federal databases. Create your account and test our proprietary risk calculator on addresses you're considering. Your first Essential report is free, giving you flood zones, environmental concerns, climate projections, and insurance implications in one clear document.

Share this with your contractor, inspector, and insurance agent—professionals who join our partner network can integrate these reports into their client services. The digital toolkit includes negotiation templates, cost calculators, and documentation guides. The video masterclass shows real examples of buyers using property intelligence to negotiate successfully. Get equipped with data that creates leverage, not just information.

Chapter 4

Negotiating Flood Costs Before You Close

Sarah thought she was buying a simple $410,000 family home in a quiet coastal town. The photos were beautiful, the street felt safe, and the only line that made her pause was small: "Property located in FEMA Zone AE." Her agent said, "Lots of homes here are," and moved on.

Sarah did not.

She pulled real quotes. Flood insurance on this home came back at $2,200 per year. A comparable home in nearby Zone X? About $800 per year. That extra $1,400 each year felt annoying until she ran the 30-year math.

$1,400 × 30 years = $42,000.

In other words, if she paid full price, she was not really buying a $410,000 home. She was buying a $452,000 home once the flood cost was baked in.

Most buyers do not feel the flood insurance pain until after they sign. By then, the seller has moved on and you own the bill.

When she asked the seller to talk, the first response was predictable: "It's never flooded. Everyone here pays flood insurance."

Instead of arguing, Sarah sent a short, calm email. She attached the FEMA map, both insurance quotes, and a one-page summary that showed the $42,000 long-term difference. Then she did what most buyers never do—she turned that number into a specific, reasonable request.

Her offer was simple: a **$30,000 price reduction** plus a **$600 seller credit** to cover the elevation certificate. She would absorb the rest of the risk and the ongoing premiums.

After two days of back-and-forth, the seller agreed.

Net outcome: Sarah shifted $30,600 of that $42,000 flood burden back to the seller, and still got the home she loved.

This chapter shows you how to do the same with your own numbers, on any property in any flood zone.

The Hidden Penalty

Most buyers do not feel the flood insurance pain until it is too late. They fall in love with the kitchen, the view, or the school zone, then go under contract. Only after the lender orders the flood determination do the real numbers show up.

National flood insurance averages run around $900-$1,100 per year, but high-risk zones regularly jump to $1,700+ in coastal areas. In the same market, a low-risk Zone X home might cost $650-$800 per year.

□ **RED FLAG #1:** A $900 difference per year equals $27,000 over a 30-year mortgage. A $1,500 gap equals $45,000. Most buyers never run this math before they sign.

That gap seems small month to month but huge over time. Add Risk Rating 2.0's allowed 18% annual premium increases until a property hits its "true risk" price, and many buyers are looking at $50,000-$100,000 more in lifetime insurance costs than a similar home outside the flood zone.

□ **ACTION STEP 1:** Before making any offer, verify the property's FEMA flood zone using official maps at FEMA.gov or your county's GIS system.

Flood insurance is not a "nice to have" when a home sits in a Special Flood Hazard Area. Federally regulated lenders **must require it**. If FEMA maps your property into Zone A, AE, or V, you cannot just skip coverage to save money. No insurance, no loan.

From the lender's view, your flood insurance premium is part of your monthly payment. Higher premiums mean higher debt-to-income ratios, which can limit how much house you qualify for.

On the resale side, flood zones create a clear price and speed penalty. National research shows flood-zone discounts in the 4%-10% range, and specific markets like Miami-Dade have seen new flood-zone designations knock values down around 14% compared to similar homes outside the zone.

A $400,000 non-flood home might go for $340,000-$380,000 once flood risk is priced in. That gap follows you into every future offer.

Time on market stretches too. In many Florida markets, flood-zone homes sit an extra 21 days or more compared to similar non-flood listings. That means more carrying costs for the seller and more leverage for any serious buyer.

The question is not whether to negotiate—it is **how** to negotiate effectively.

Turning Risk Into Numbers

To negotiate flood costs, you first turn vague risk into a clear price tag. Use this simple formula on every flood-zone property:

Base flood-zone premium: $________ per year **Comparable non-flood premium:** $________ per year **Annual difference:** $________ per year **Annual difference × 30 years:** $________ **Elevation certificate (one-time):** $________ **Planned mitigation work:** $________ **Total documented flood cost:** $________

Real Example: A buyer in a FEMA AE zone received a quote of $2,200 per year. A comparable home in nearby Zone X was about $800 per year.

- Annual difference: $1,400
- 30-year impact: $42,000
- Elevation certificate: $600
- Planned utility elevation and vents: $8,000
- **Total documented flood cost: $50,600**

The buyer presented this worksheet to the seller and requested a $30,000 price reduction plus the $600 certificate cost. After negotiation, they settled on $25,000 + $600, shifting $25,600 of that burden back to the seller.

□ **ACTION STEP 2:** Request at least three flood insurance quotes—one from the National Flood Insurance Program (NFIP) and two from private carriers. Use identical coverage limits for fair comparison.

This formula works because it forces both sides to look at **real long-term costs**, not gut feelings. Sellers respond to numbers, not complaints.

Warning Signs to Watch

Not every flood-zone property is negotiable. Watch for these warning signs:

□ **RED FLAG #2:** The seller refuses any discussion about flood-related costs. A firm "no negotiation" stance often signals they know future buyers will face the same concerns.

□ **RED FLAG #3:** Insurance quotes exceed $2,200-$2,400 per year (the common AE-zone range), especially when comparable Zone X homes are closer to $800. This gap becomes unsustainable over time.

□ **ACTION STEP 3:** Access FEMA's public claims database to identify any past flood events tied to the property. Prior claims are public record and may affect your premium.

Also walk if the property shows prior FEMA claims or sits in a high-risk V zone with limited mitigation options. If no vents, elevation, or utility upgrades can reduce premiums, long-term ownership becomes difficult.

Your walk-away number should equal the annual premium difference × 30 years. Compare that to expected appreciation and only proceed if long-term value outweighs long-term cost.

Your Five-Step Execution Plan

Once you have your numbers, follow this execution timeline:

□ **ACTION STEP 4 (Week 1):** Include a flood insurance contingency in your offer. Use simple language: "Subject to acceptable flood insurance costs based on buyer's lender requirements."

□ **ACTION STEP 5 (Week 1):** Request the seller's current insurance declarations page. If their policy is grandfathered or more favorable, you may be able to assume it.

□ **ACTION STEP 6 (Week 2):** Order an elevation certificate if the seller does not have one. This may reduce the premium or confirm the lender's requirement. Cost: typically $500-$800.

□ **ACTION STEP 7 (Week 2):** Organize your findings into a simple written cost analysis. Include the 30-year projection, elevation certificate cost, and mitigation estimates. Present this professional packet to the seller.

□ **ACTION STEP 8 (Week 2-3):** Submit your analysis and request a direct conversation. Lead with data first: "Here are the documented costs. Based on this, we're requesting..." Keep the discussion focused on lender requirements and long-term ownership costs.

Sellers respond to professional, documented requests. Buyers who show up with real numbers and a clear ask get better results than buyers who complain without proof.

What Success Looks Like

A successful flood negotiation is not about "getting a deal." It is about keeping long-term ownership costs under control.

Consider this real outcome: A buyer in a FEMA AE zone received a $2,200 annual quote, compared to $800 for a similar Zone X home. Instead of absorbing the $1,400 yearly difference, the buyer documented the 30-year impact ($42,000), added a $600 elevation certificate, plus $8,000 in recommended mitigation.

With clear numbers, the seller agreed to a **$25,000 price reduction** and a **$600 elevation certificate credit**—a $25,600 immediate benefit.

Once mitigation was completed, the new insurance quote dropped by roughly $150 per month, creating an additional $54,000 in savings over 30 years.

Total benefit: approximately $79,600.

That is money the buyer keeps, not money paid to insurance carriers. Even better, the property became more attractive for future resale because mitigation work improved its long-term risk profile.

A home that costs less to insure—and has documentation to prove it—commands stronger offers and reduces buyer hesitation. Flood negotiation is not just a short-term win; it protects you when it is your turn to sell.

Chapter 4 Key Takeaways

□ A $900 annual flood insurance gap equals $27,000 over 30 years—run the math before you sign

□ Use the Flood Cost Formula to turn vague risk into a clear, documented price tag

□ Request three quotes (NFIP + two private carriers) and compare identical coverage limits

□ Include a flood insurance contingency in your offer to preserve negotiation leverage

□ Order an elevation certificate early—it may reduce premiums or confirm lender requirements

□ Walk away if the seller refuses discussion or if premiums exceed $2,200-$2,400 with no mitigation options

□ Present a professional cost analysis with 30-year projections to strengthen your negotiation position

□ Successful negotiation can shift $25,000-$50,000+ in lifetime flood costs back to the seller

----

Chapter Resources

Feel free to skip ahead if you'd like to continue reading.

Flood negotiation starts with accurate data. Before you negotiate flood insurance costs or FEMA zone appeals, you need the actual numbers. Visit **HomeDataReports.com** to pull detailed flood risk analysis for any address—Base Flood Elevation calculations, historical flood claims data, insurance cost estimates, and zone verification all in one report. Our risk calculator shows you immediately if a property sits in Special Flood Hazard Areas requiring mandatory coverage. Create your free account and get your first Essential report that includes comprehensive flood analysis.

Download the Chrome extension to check flood zones while browsing properties—before you fall in love with a house and discover $6,000 annual insurance costs during escrow. Share this tool with your insurance agent and realtor. When they join our partner referral network, they can provide flood data to clients before negotiations start, not after contracts are signed. The video masterclass includes real examples of buyers negotiating flood-related concessions using documented FEMA data.

Chapter 5

Negotiating Fire Risk When Insurance Gets Expensive

When Paper Reveals the Real Problem

The first red flag was not fire—it was paper.

A thick stack of non-renewal letters sat on the seller's kitchen counter. Their longtime carrier had pulled out. Two neighbors were forced into the state's high-risk pool. Another was paying more for insurance than property taxes.

Your target home sits in the Wildland-Urban Interface—trees at the back fence, open space beyond. On paper, it looks like a dream. Until your insurance broker makes calls and discovers what the letters mean.

Out of twelve carriers, only two will quote. Both at three times the standard rate. Your broker's email: "Best available: $6,000 per year. Comparable non-WUI homes: $1,800."

That $4,200 annual gap becomes $126,000 over thirty years—before a single tree ever burns.

California's FAIR Plan has exploded to 645,987 policies, up 169% in four years. Multiple western states see 25–300% premium increases. Nearly 45% of agents report buyers walking away because they cannot secure affordable coverage.

When you raise this, the seller responds: "We've never had problems."

So you bring data instead of fear. You document carrier withdrawals, show side-by-side quotes, and present written estimates for ember-resistant vents and defensible space that could qualify for 15–25% discounts.

The seller agrees to a $45,000 price reduction plus $15,000 credit for fire hardening. You complete the upgrades, your premium drops 25%, and the long-term cost becomes manageable.

The real issue isn't whether a property can burn—it's whether you can afford to insure it for the next 30 years.

The Insurance Crisis

State Farm non-renewed 72,000 California policies. Allstate stopped writing new policies in 2022. Farmers, American National, and Chubb withdrew from specific WUI zones. In some fire-exposed regions, buyers find only one or two carriers willing to quote—sometimes none.

> □ **RED FLAG #1:** If only the FAIR Plan will cover the property, that's an availability crisis, not a pricing issue.

Even when coverage exists, premiums have spiked. Colorado saw a 57.9% increase between 2018 and 2023. California rates are projected to rise 21% in 2025. High-WUI homeowners now receive $4,000–$6,000 quotes compared to $1,500–$2,000 for non-WUI properties.

California's FAIR Plan averages $3,200 per year, often requiring separate wraparound policies that raise total costs higher. A $4,000 annual premium difference over thirty years equals $120,000 in additional carrying costs.

Despite this crisis, listing prices in WUI neighborhoods still reflect pre-2020 assumptions. Sellers are unaware because they have grandfathered policies or haven't received non-renewal notices yet. Buyers discover the issue after going under contract, creating financial pressure and negotiation opportunities.

Homes in high-risk WUI zones remain on market 15–30% longer than comparable non-WUI properties.

Fire Hardening as Leverage

Fire hardening reduces a home's vulnerability to ember attacks and radiant heat. These upgrades unlock premium discounts from insurers. The key: **fire hardening is measurable, documentable, and financially quantifiable.**

Essential upgrades:

Ember-Resistant Vents ($1,500–$3,000): Block ember entry while maintaining airflow. Premium reduction: 5–10%.

Non-Combustible Roofing ($8,000–$15,000): Class A rated materials. Premium reduction: 10–15%.

Gutter Guards ($1,000–$2,500): Prevent debris accumulation. Premium reduction: 3–5%.

Defensible Space ($2,000–$5,000): Clear vegetation within 5 feet (Zone 0), maintain low-fuel landscaping within 30 feet (Zone 1), manage brush within 100 feet (Zone 2). Premium reduction: 10–20% (highest impact).

Fire hardening measures costing $15,000–$25,000 can reduce premiums by 20–30%, paying for themselves within 10–15 years.

Programs like Firewise USA and IBHS provide third-party certification ($300–$500) that streamlines insurer discount approvals. In California, Colorado, and Oregon, some insurers won't write WUI policies unless the property meets minimum hardening standards.

□ **ACTION STEP:** Request a Fire Risk Assessment from a certified specialist before making an offer ($300–$600). This identifies required upgrades and estimates insurance savings.

When to Walk Away

□ **RED FLAG #2:** Walk away if zero standard-market carriers will quote, if FAIR Plan is the only option, if fire hardening exceeds $50,000, or if major fires occurred within five miles in the past three years.

If the seller refuses any negotiation on fire-related costs or if the property experienced carrier non-renewal within the past year, these signal transaction problems ahead. Some properties cannot be made economically insurable through mitigation alone.

The Five-Step Negotiation

Step 1: Document Insurance Availability (Week 1)

Contact three independent brokers. Request quotes from standard-market carriers. Document which carriers declined and why. Obtain written declination notices.

Step 2: Research Fire Hardening Costs (Week 1–2)

Get written contractor estimates for ember-resistant vents, gutter guards, defensible space, and any needed roof or window upgrades. Request documentation showing how each qualifies for discounts.

Step 3: Calculate Cost Differential (Week 2)

Compare the property's insurance cost to non-WUI homes. Calculate the 30-year impact. This becomes your negotiation foundation.

□ **ACTION STEP:** Calculate the 30-year insurance cost differential and present it to the seller as documented financial impact.

Step 4: Present Multiple Options (Week 2)

Offer three structures:

- **Option A:** Full price reduction to offset insurance costs
- **Option B:** Partial price reduction plus seller credit for mitigation
- **Option C:** Seller completes certified fire hardening plus partial price reduction

Sample script: "Based on documented carrier availability and long-term cost differences, we're requesting adjustments that reflect current underwriting standards. Here are three options that work for both of us..."

Step 5: Execute Agreement (Week 2–3)

Formalize every detail in the contract. For seller credits, ensure they're clearly listed and reflect contractor estimates. Begin Firewise or IBHS certification within 30 days of closing.

□ **ACTION STEP:** Start certification process immediately after closing for fastest discount approvals.

Understanding Risk Tolerance

Walk away when:

- Zero standard carriers quote
- FAIR Plan is the only option
- Major fire within five miles (past three years)
- Hardening costs exceed $50,000
- Seller refuses negotiation

Proceed with caution if:

- Two to three carriers will insure at elevated premiums
- Hardening can reduce costs by 20%+
- You plan to hold 10+ years
- Seller shares mitigation costs
- Post-hardening premiums fall within your acceptable range

Success Story

A California buyer facing $6,000 annual premiums (versus $1,800 for non-WUI comparables) documented the 30-year differential and mitigation costs. The negotiation resulted in a $45,000 price reduction plus $15,000 seller credit for fire hardening.

After completing upgrades, the buyer qualified for 25% premium reduction—$1,500 per year in savings, or $45,000 over thirty years. **Total negotiated benefit: $105,000.** More importantly, the certified fire hardening made the property more marketable for future resale.

When you understand insurance availability and mitigation pathways, you can turn a crisis into meaningful leverage.

Moving Forward

Fire-risk negotiation teaches a powerful lesson: data transforms complex situations into leverage. But wildfire is only one regional risk. Next, we shift to earthquake risk.

The contrast matters. **Fire risk affects insurance availability**—carriers may decline policies entirely. **Earthquake risk affects insurance decisions**—coverage is optional while structural vulnerability is not.

For fire, you negotiate hardening costs with the seller. For earthquakes, you negotiate based on engineering requirements that influence the property's stability.

Both require data—but the strategies differ significantly.

Chapter 5 Key Takeaways

□ Insurance availability—not just cost—is the primary fire-risk challenge in WUI zones

□ Major carriers have withdrawn, creating "insurance deserts" where only 1–2 carriers will quote

□ A $4,200/year premium gap equals $126,000 over 30 years

□ Fire hardening ($15,000–$25,000) can reduce premiums by 15–30%

□ Five-step process: Document availability, research hardening costs, calculate differentials, present options, execute agreements

□ Walk away if zero carriers quote, hardening exceeds $50,000, or recent major fires occurred nearby

□ Successful negotiations combine price reductions with seller credits for mitigation work

----

Chapter Resources

Feel free to skip ahead if you'd like to continue reading.

Wildfire negotiation requires wildfire data. You can't negotiate insurance costs or fire mitigation expenses without understanding the actual risk exposure. Generate comprehensive wildfire risk reports at **HomeDataReports.com** —our platform aggregates CalFire data, USFS fire history, and Wildland-Urban Interface designations into clear risk profiles. The proprietary risk calculator evaluates fire exposure instantly, showing you whether properties face insurability challenges before you make offers. Create your free account today and get your first Essential report covering fire risk, evacuation routes, and historical burn patterns.

Install our Chrome extension to research fire zones while browsing mountain properties. Tell your insurance agent about our partner program—agents who join can access detailed fire risk data for accurate quoting and coverage availability before clients waste time on uninsurable properties. The digital toolkit includes fire mitigation cost calculators and defensible space templates. When wildfire insurance costs become negotiation points, you'll have the documented data that creates leverage.

Chapter 6

Negotiating Earthquake Concerns

The first clue was not a crack in the wall—it was the inspector's voice from the crawl space.

"Your cripple wall down here is bare studs," he said. "And these bolts? There aren't nearly enough of them."

On paper, the 1940s bungalow looked charming: tree-lined street, walkable neighborhood, solid price. In person, the inspection report told a different story. The raised foundation had an unreinforced cripple wall and inadequate foundation bolting. A structural engineer confirmed what the buyer suspected: a proper Brace + Bolt retrofit would run $18,000.

Then came the second number: an earthquake insurance quote of $2,400 per year—with a high deductible that still left the buyer on the hook for tens of thousands.

The seller's response was familiar: "This place has stood for 80 years. It'll be fine."

Insurance doesn't keep a house on its foundation during shaking. Retrofitting does.

Instead of arguing, the buyer separated the issues. The engineer's report showed a clear structural deficiency. That made retrofit a safety necessity, not a preference. Earthquake insurance was a financial decision the buyer could make after closing.

So the buyer requested an $18,000 credit tied specifically to seismic retrofit work, dropping any request related to earthquake insurance. The seller agreed. The retrofit happened, and the home's weakness was addressed before move-in.

That single choice turned a vague worry into a clear, structural win.

Here's how to negotiate the structure, not the insurance.

Why Buyers Get This Wrong

Most buyers treat insurance and structural safety as the same thing. If they can get an earthquake policy, they feel protected. But insurance does not keep a house on its foundation during shaking. Retrofitting does.

Structural engineers and federal studies show that unretrofitted pre-1960 homes experience higher damage rates. In past earthquakes, cripple-wall failures accounted for about two-thirds of the worst residential losses in events like Northridge. Insurance can help pay for rebuilding afterward, but it cannot stop a cripple wall from buckling.

□ **RED FLAG #1:** When a seller says "This place has stood for decades," that's not proof of safety. Most pre-1960 homes have never experienced a major earthquake test. Structural deficiencies exist whether or not the house has shaken yet.

That gap between perception and reality is where negotiations go sideways. Buyers assume they'll just get earthquake insurance and never ask what's holding the house up. Sellers talk about coverage instead of structural weaknesses. The result is a fuzzy conversation about premiums, not bolts and bracing.

Typical Brace + Bolt work for a pre-1960 raised-foundation home runs $5,000–$10,000. More complex projects with chimney reinforcement can reach $15,000–$25,000. That's real money, but it's also the cost of addressing a deficiency modern building codes would never allow.

Retrofit work is more like repairing a cracked foundation. It's core to the home's ability to withstand shaking.

Sellers often push back with "It's not required." What they mean is, "The law hasn't forced me to fix this yet," not "The structure is safe."

Meanwhile, buyers treat retrofit decisions like granite countertops—nice to have, but negotiable. That framing is backwards. Retrofit work is like repairing a cracked foundation. It's core to the home's ability to withstand shaking and remain habitable.

□ **RED FLAG #2:** Earthquake insurance is expensive—annual premiums in California run $1,000–$2,000 with deductibles of 5–25% of the home's value. On a $500,000 home, that's a $25,000–$125,000 deductible before coverage activates. Only 10–15% of California homeowners carry earthquake insurance. Don't let insurance costs distract from retrofit needs.

Separate structural safety, which travels with the property, from insurance decisions, which change from owner to owner. Your negotiation focuses on structural integrity, not insurance premiums.

Building Your Retrofit Case

Negotiating seismic retrofit costs starts with a clear scope. You're turning vague "earthquake risk" into a specific repair list the seller can react to.

For a typical pre-1960 raised-foundation home:

Foundation bolting: $1,000–$5,000. Secures the house frame to the foundation.

Cripple wall bracing: $1,000–$3,000. Adds plywood shear panels in the crawl space.

Chimney reinforcement: $1,000–$3,000 per chimney.

Soft-story work: $10,000–$27,000 for small residential buildings.

□ **ACTION STEP 1:** Hire a structural engineer with seismic experience. Request photos, measurements, and notes on deficiencies. Get this done during your first 7–10 days of escrow.

Regional costs vary. Bay Area retrofits run $3,200–$7,500 for single-family homes. Los Angeles sees $3,000–$10,000 for Brace + Bolt work. Seattle and Portland range from $4,000–$10,000.

Sarah's 1950s Home in Vallejo, CA

Sarah found a 1,500-square-foot raised-foundation home at $425,000. Her structural engineer noted unbraced cripple walls and bolts spaced 24 inches apart—code requires 12–16 inches. Retrofit estimate: $5,500.

The seller resisted. Sarah's agent explained the lender would require a 120% escrow holdback ($6,600) if not resolved—more expensive for the seller.

The seller compromised: $3,000 price reduction plus $2,500 in closing credits, totaling $5,500. Sarah completed the retrofit post-closing for $5,200. Total out-of-pocket: $0.

Once you have your inspection report and contractor estimates, present three options:

Option 1: Retrofit credit. The seller reduces the price by the retrofit amount. You handle the work after closing.

Option 2: Seller completes work. The seller hires a contractor and finishes before closing. You verify completion with permit sign-off.

Option 3: Escrow holdback. The seller holds funds in escrow (typically 120% of costs). Work is completed post-closing, and remaining funds are released.

□ **ACTION STEP 2:** Assemble a retrofit packet: inspection findings, contractor estimates, photos, and local ordinance information. Complete this during week two of escrow.

When presenting your request, lead with structural safety. Show the inspector's photos, summarize the deficiencies, attach contractor estimates. Make the separation explicit: "This request is solely for structural safety work. We'll evaluate earthquake insurance after closing."

Retrofit work is a structural necessity that travels with the property. Insurance is a personal financial decision that changes owner to owner. Never combine them.

When to Walk Away

Walk away when a seller refuses any retrofit discussion despite documented deficiencies, especially in pre-1960 homes. If retrofit estimates exceed $40,000–$50,000, the structural risk may be too high.

□ **RED FLAG #3:** Unreinforced masonry chimneys with stability concerns or soft-story configurations without a clear retrofit plan justify stepping back. A seller's unwillingness to engage signals limited flexibility.

Proceed with caution when a seller is open to negotiating but won't meet the full request. If the home only needs standard bolting and bracing ($5,000–$10,000), the pathway is clearer.

□ **ACTION STEP 3:** Calculate your maximum acceptable out-of-pocket cost before negotiating. If the seller won't cover retrofit work and remaining costs exceed your budget, walk away. Structural safety is non-negotiable.

Your Five-Step Timeline

Step 1: Inspection (Days 1–10)

Hire an inspector or structural engineer with seismic experience. Request evaluation of foundation bolting, cripple-wall bracing, chimney stability, and soft-story characteristics. Get photos, measurements, and notes.

☐ **ACTION STEP 4:** Request itemized estimates from two to three licensed seismic retrofit contractors. Verify license status and retrofit experience.

Step 2: Get Quotes (Days 10–20)

Contact licensed contractors. Request line-by-line estimates showing pricing for bolting, bracing, chimney work, and permit costs. Complete this within 7–10 days of receiving your inspection report.

Step 3: Build Case (Week 2)

Assemble a retrofit packet with inspector findings, contractor estimates, photos, and ordinance information. Reference comparable homes that completed retrofits. Highlight typical regional costs to show your request aligns with market norms.

Lead with structural safety, not risk predictions. Keep your tone factual.

Step 4: Present Request (Week 2)

Show inspector photos, summarize deficiencies, attach estimates. Explain retrofit benefits any owner and is tied to physical condition—not insurance. Make it explicit: "This is solely for structural work. We'll evaluate insurance after closing."

☐ **ACTION STEP 5:** Present your request in week two, before inspection contingency expires. Keep tone factual.

Step 5: Negotiate (Weeks 2–3)

Present multiple options: retrofit credit, seller-completed work, or escrow holdback. Clarify what each covers and expected timelines. If seller completes work, specify licensed contractor and permit sign-off required. Document everything in a contract amendment.

□ **ACTION STEP 6:** Document the final agreement in writing. Specify costs, responsibilities, timelines, and permit requirements before contingencies are removed.

What You Gain

A successful retrofit negotiation strengthens your entire investment. Consider the earlier scenario: a pre-1960 home with inadequate bolting and unbraced cripple walls. The buyer presented an engineer's report and contractor estimates totaling $18,000.

The seller agreed to an $18,000 retrofit credit. That ensured the home could be properly anchored and braced, improving performance under lateral forces and addressing collapse patterns found in older wood-frame construction.

The real win was confidence in the home's integrity—something every future owner will appreciate.

The long-term reward: enhanced structural safety plus an estimated $20,000–$30,000 property value increase once retrofit is complete.

Because the buyer kept insurance separate, they maintained complete flexibility to evaluate coverage later. The real win was confidence in the home's integrity—something every future owner will appreciate.

Mike's 1940s Home in Seattle

Mike found a 2,000-square-foot raised-foundation home at $625,000. His engineer noted unbraced cripple walls and inadequate bolting. Retrofit estimate: $6,200.

The seller claimed the property "survived 1949" (a modest shake). Mike's lender required retrofit for loan approval.

The seller agreed to $4,000 price reduction plus $2,500 closing credits, totaling $6,500. Mike completed retrofit for $6,100 and got earthquake insurance at $1,050 yearly with 15% retrofit discount (versus $1,250 without). Over 10 years, the retrofit is cost-neutral. Mike's out-of-pocket: $0.

This book isn't about scaring you away from homes. It's about giving you information to make decisions right for YOU. What matters is that you KNOW before you buy—not discover it after closing.

Chapter 6 Key Takeaways

☐ **Separate retrofit from insurance.** Retrofit is structural necessity. Insurance is personal financial choice.

☐ **Typical costs:** $5,000–$10,000 for Brace + Bolt; $15,000–$25,000 for complex projects; $10,000–$27,000 for soft-story work.

☐ **Red flags:** Sellers refusing retrofit discussion; estimates exceeding $40,000–$50,000; unreinforced masonry chimneys; soft-story without clear plan.

☐ **Options:** Retrofit credit, seller-completed work, or escrow holdback.

☐ **Lead with structural safety.** Show photos, deficiencies, estimates. Frame as value-added improvement.

☐ **Timeline:** Days 1–10 (inspection), Days 10–20 (quotes), Week 2 (build case, present), Weeks 2–3 (negotiate).

☐ **Reward:** Structural safety plus $20,000–$30,000 property value increase.

Chapter Resources

Feel free to skip ahead if you'd like to continue reading.

Seismic negotiation demands seismic data. Before you negotiate foundation retrofits or earthquake insurance, get the actual USGS hazard assessment for your target property. Visit **HomeDataReports.com** to generate reports covering seismic risk, liquefaction potential, fault line proximity, and building code compliance for any U.S. address. Our risk calculator evaluates earthquake exposure using the same probabilistic models professionals rely on. Create your account and receive your first Essential report free—including detailed seismic analysis that reveals risks inspectors won't catch.

Download the Chrome extension to check earthquake hazards while browsing properties in California, Pacific Northwest, or other seismic regions. Share this with your structural engineer and home inspector—when they join our partner network, they can provide clients with seismic data before inspections, improving assessment accuracy. The video masterclass shows how buyers use earthquake data to negotiate retrofit costs and insurance requirements. Get the foundation analysis before you negotiate the foundation work.

Chapter 7

Negotiating Environmental Issues

The problem did not start with a scary headline. It started with a small note on a map: the property sat 0.3 miles from an EPA Superfund site with historical groundwater contamination. The home itself looked clean. The lawn was perfect. The listing disclosures were quiet. So the buyer did what this book keeps telling you to do—verify instead of guess.

A Phase I Environmental Site Assessment, roughly $2,200–$3,500 in most residential cases, flagged a recognized environmental condition and recommended limited subsurface testing. The buyer authorized a Phase II investigation, typically $8,000–$15,000 for a standard residential scope, focused on shallow soil samples near the backyard and side yard. Lab results showed elevated lead levels above residential screening standards.

The home looked perfect. But 18 inches below the surface, the soil told a different story. Phase II testing revealed lead contamination that would have cost me $18,000 to fix—or $50,000 in legal exposure if I'd discovered it after closing.

Remediation contractors estimated $12,000–$18,000 to remove contaminated soil, backfill with clean material, and document the work for regulators and future buyers. The seller's first instinct was to offer a $10,000 credit and call it resolved.

The buyer treated it differently. Instead of arguing about feelings, they negotiated in layers: first, an $18,000 credit to fully cover the high end of the remediation range; second, a detailed environmental indemnity clause that kept the seller on the hook for any pre-existing contamination claims; third, an updated disclosure package and a third-party monitoring plan to document clean closure for the next owner.

By the time the deal closed, the numbers, the legal risk, and the future resale story were all addressed. The buyer did not walk away from the property. They walked into it with eyes open, cleanup funded, and liability clearly allocated in writing.

This is not about panic; it is about process.

Why Environmental Issues Demand Precision

Environmental issues require a level of precision and protection that ordinary property defects simply do not demand. Unlike a roof leak or outdated electrical panel, contamination carries hidden financial, legal, and regulatory consequences that extend far beyond the visible boundaries of a home.

> □ **RED FLAG #1:** Under CERCLA (Superfund law), liability often follows ownership—not responsibility. Buyers can inherit cleanup obligations for contamination they never created, even from facilities located blocks away.

The Hidden Liability

Environmental contamination is rarely obvious from a visual inspection. Soil can look clean while containing lead, petroleum hydrocarbons, PFAS compounds, or volatile organic chemicals left behind decades earlier. The challenge is that liability often follows ownership—not responsibility.

In multiple Superfund cases, residential owners were named as potentially responsible parties even when contamination originated from commercial operations several blocks away. One documented case involved homeowners being held partially liable for groundwater cleanup costs exceeding $30 million after purchasing property near a metal finishing facility.

> Without proper due diligence, buyers can inherit obligations they never created—obligations that can persist for years and cost more than the home itself.

The Discovery Problem

Most buyers never run an EPA Superfund or Toxic Release Inventory search, and many do not know these databases exist. As a result, contamination is often discovered only after closing—usually during renovations, landscaping, or insurance inspections.

More than 30% of contamination discoveries occur during refinancing or resale, not during the original purchase. By then, the buyer owns both the property and the liability.

Industry data shows that Phase I Environmental Site Assessments routinely identify historical uses buyers were unaware of. The gap is even clearer in Phase II testing: although it ranges from $8,000 to $15,000 on residential properties, it commonly prevents buyers from unknowingly assuming $50,000 to $500,000+ in cleanup exposure.

Former dry cleaners, gas stations, textile plants, and industrial workshops leave behind solvents and petroleum products that remain in soil and groundwater for decades. Even proximity matters—homes within one mile of a Superfund site typically sell at a 5–8% discount, while properties near industrial facilities appreciate more slowly due to market perception.

□ **RED FLAG #2:** Properties previously used as gas stations, dry cleaners, automotive shops, or industrial operations carry significantly higher contamination risk. Always run EPA database searches before making an offer.

The Dual Risk

Environmental issues create two simultaneous threats. First is the financial risk: remediation can range from $12,000 for shallow soil removal, to $50,000–$150,000 for leaking underground storage tanks, to more than $250,000 when PFAS or chlorinated solvents require long-term extraction and monitoring.

A price reduction alone does not protect against environmental liabilities. Buyers need both financial adjustments AND a legally enforceable indemnity that assigns responsibility for historical contamination to the seller.

Second is the legal risk: once contamination is discovered, owners may face obligations under state environmental laws, potential contribution claims, and disclosure duties affecting future resale.

A price reduction alone does not protect against these liabilities. Buyers need both financial adjustments (credits, holdbacks, or reduced purchase price) and a legally enforceable environmental indemnity. Without this dual protection, a buyer may save money upfront but remain exposed to significant downstream costs and legal responsibilities.

How to Negotiate Environmental Contamination

Environmental negotiations work only when buyers follow a structured, evidence-based sequence. Unlike cosmetic issues, contamination requires verified data, documented cost ranges, and legally enforceable protections.

Step 1: Search Federal Databases

Before making an offer, search the EPA's Superfund, Toxic Release Inventory, and brownfield databases. Check FEMA's environmental layers and state environmental agency records. Identify any sites within one mile of the property that may pose contamination risk.

☐ **ACTION STEP 1:** Run EPA database searches at Envirofacts (epa.gov) and your state environmental agency website. Document any facilities within 1 mile of the property.

Look for historical uses that suggest possible contamination—especially former gas stations, dry cleaners, automotive repair shops, or industrial operations. Document findings with screenshots and addresses for your negotiation file.

Timeline: Complete searches before making offer.

Step 2: Include Phase I Contingency

Once preliminary concerns are identified, determine whether a Phase I Environmental Site Assessment is necessary. Include a Phase I contingency in your offer so you can withdraw or renegotiate based on the findings.

☐ **ACTION STEP 2:** Add Phase I contingency language to your purchase offer: "Buyer reserves the right to obtain a Phase I Environmental Site Assessment at Buyer's expense and renegotiate or withdraw based on findings."

This ensures environmental due diligence is built into the negotiation rather than addressed after acceptance.

Timeline: Decide Phase I needs during offer negotiation.

Step 3: Phase I Assessment

Hire a qualified environmental consultant to complete the Phase I, which typically ranges from $2,200–$3,500 for standard properties. The consultant will review records, conduct interviews, and perform a site walk to identify Recognized Environmental Conditions.

If the Phase I recommends Phase II testing ($8,000–$15,000), authorize it promptly. Every documented concern becomes negotiation leverage when discussing credits, price adjustments, or indemnity language with the seller.

□ **ACTION STEP 3:** Request three references from environmental consultants before hiring. Verify they carry E&O insurance and have completed similar residential assessments.

Timeline: Complete Phase I during weeks 1–2 of escrow.

Step 4: Quantify & Negotiate

If Phase II confirms contamination or if the Phase I identifies significant risk, obtain remediation estimates from licensed environmental contractors. These estimates often define cleanup ranges such as $12,000 for shallow soil removal or $25,000–$50,000+ for more complex cases.

Work with your attorney to draft an environmental indemnity clause that protects you from future claims tied to pre-existing contamination. Present a dual request to the seller: a financial adjustment for documented cleanup costs and legal protection through indemnity.

□ **ACTION STEP 4:** Request written remediation estimates from at least two licensed contractors. Use the higher estimate as your negotiation baseline.

□ **RED FLAG #3:** If the seller refuses to provide an environmental indemnity clause, the risk becomes unpredictable. Decline deals where sellers won't accept responsibility for pre-existing contamination.

Offer structured options such as price reduction, remediation credits, or escrow holdbacks.

Timeline: Begin negotiations in weeks 2–3 of escrow.

Step 5: Formalize Protection

Once terms are agreed upon, ensure all protections are incorporated into the purchase contract. The environmental indemnity should clearly assign responsibility for pre-existing contamination to the seller. Require the seller to update disclosures to reflect all environmental findings.

□ **ACTION STEP 5:** Have your attorney review the environmental indemnity language before signing. Standard contract language often fails to address contamination liability adequately.

If remediation will occur before closing, define the scope, timeline, and need for clearance documents such as "No Further Action" letters. If remediation will occur after closing, confirm that funds, indemnity provisions, and monitoring requirements are fully documented.

□ **ACTION STEP 6:** Require seller to provide copies of all environmental reports, remediation plans, and regulatory correspondence at closing. These documents are essential for future resale.

Timeline: Finalize documentation during weeks 3–4 of escrow.

When to Walk Away, When to Negotiate

Environmental decisions require a clear understanding of what is acceptable risk and what is beyond a reasonable threshold.

Walk Away If:

Walk away when contamination is confirmed on-site above regulatory action levels, especially for lead, petroleum hydrocarbons, chlorinated solvents, or PFAS compounds. If a Phase I recommends Phase II but the seller refuses further testing, the risk becomes unpredictable.

□ **RED FLAG #4:** Properties requiring long-term or indefinite monitoring exceed reasonable buyer exposure. If remediation cannot achieve regulatory closure within 12–24 months, walk away.

Decline the deal if the seller rejects an environmental indemnity clause or if remediation estimates exceed $50,000–$100,000 with no guaranteed regulatory closure.

Proceed With Caution If:

Proceed cautiously when contamination is nearby but not confirmed on-site, or when Phase I is clean but proximity raises concern. Move forward only if the seller provides full indemnity, a meaningful price adjustment, and documented transparency.

Establish your maximum acceptable environmental liability in advance. Know your walk-away number before you start negotiating.

Ensure remediation, if needed, is one-time, clearly scoped, and capable of obtaining regulatory clearance.

The Reward: Protection on Both Fronts

Real Example: Lead Contamination Negotiation

A property located near a historical industrial site triggered a Phase I assessment that identified a potential environmental concern. Phase II sampling revealed elevated lead levels in the side yard. Cleanup estimates ranged from $12,000 to $18,000.

The buyer negotiated a $15,000 remediation credit to cover the high end of the cost range. More importantly, the buyer secured a seller-funded environmental indemnity covering all pre-existing contamination, plus updated disclosures and contractor documentation.

Result: The credit handled the cleanup, the indemnity handled any unknown future findings, and the documentation ensured that future buyers would see a properly remediated and fully cleared property. Combined protection: financial security + legal protection + improved marketability.

A strong environmental negotiation does more than reduce the purchase price—it eliminates uncertainty and positions the buyer for long-term security.

The combined result is financial protection, legal security, and improved marketability. This dual-layer protection is the true reward of environmental due diligence: you control cost, eliminate liability, and gain peace of mind knowing the property has been evaluated professionally and thoroughly.

Chapter 7 Key Takeaways

□ Environmental contamination is rarely visible—Phase I and Phase II testing ($2,200–$15,000) prevents assuming $50,000–$500,000+ in cleanup liability

□ Under CERCLA, liability follows ownership, not responsibility—buyers can inherit cleanup obligations from contamination they never created

□ Dual protection is essential: negotiate BOTH financial adjustments (credits, price reductions) AND environmental indemnity clauses

□ Search EPA databases (Superfund, TRI) BEFORE making offers—former gas stations, dry cleaners, and industrial sites carry significantly higher risk

□ Walk away if: contamination confirmed on-site above action levels, seller refuses Phase II testing, or seller rejects indemnity language

□ If remediation exceeds $50,000–$100,000 or requires indefinite monitoring, the risk exceeds reasonable buyer exposure

□ Documentation is protection—require all environmental reports, clearance letters, and remediation records transfer at closing

While environmental contamination requires laboratory testing, regulatory review, and specialized assessments, the next category of risk is far more familiar to most buyers: safety issues documented during a standard home inspection. Environmental hazards may be invisible, but electrical, structural, and fire-related problems usually appear in inspection reports, photographs, and contractor evaluations. Chapter 8 shifts from chemical and historical risks to physical conditions that directly affect the home's safety and functionality—and how to use inspection findings as negotiation leverage.

Chapter Resources

Feel free to skip ahead if you'd like to continue reading.

Environmental negotiation starts with EPA data. You can't negotiate proximity to Superfund sites or contamination concerns without documented evidence. Pull comprehensive environmental reports at **HomeDataReports.com** —we aggregate EPA databases,

Toxic Release Inventory facilities, radon zone data, and brownfield sites into property-specific intelligence. Our risk calculator identifies environmental hazards within customizable radius around any address. Create your free account and get your first Essential report covering environmental risks that affect property values and long-term health.

Install the Chrome extension to research environmental concerns while browsing listings—before you schedule showings near contamination sites. Tell your realtor and appraiser about our partner referral program. Professionals who join can provide environmental data to clients during property evaluation, not after contracts are signed. The digital toolkit includes environmental risk worksheets and negotiation templates. When environmental issues become negotiation leverage, you'll have the federal data that sellers can't dispute.

Chapter 8

Negotiating Safety Concerns

The home inspector found it in the first ten minutes—the kind of note most buyers skim past in an inspection report.

"Electrical system: 60-amp service, aluminum branch wiring, multiple ungrounded outlets. Recommended correction by licensed electrician. Fire hazard."

The buyers liked the house. The price was fair. The seller's response was exactly what you would expect: "It's worked fine for 40 years."

Their electrician's estimate came back at $8,000–$12,000 to upgrade the panel, replace problem aluminum circuits, and correct ungrounded outlets. A serious number, but not life-changing.

What changed everything was the way their agent reframed the conversation.

"This isn't about what the buyers prefer," she explained. "Once this inspection is in writing, you, as the seller, now know about a documented fire hazard. If a future fire occurs and your insurer learns you knew about this and chose not to address it, they may deny the claim entirely. **That is a liability problem, not a decorating choice.**"

Once a safety hazard is documented, the seller's exposure doesn't disappear—it follows them to the next buyer and every legal conversation after.

She showed the seller how documented electrical hazards, missing smoke and carbon monoxide detectors, and other safety issues can trigger coverage denials and lawsuits that easily exceed $20,000–$100,000 in combined repair costs, legal fees, and potential damages—far more than the $10,000 credit the buyers were requesting.

The seller called an attorney, who confirmed the risk: disclosure laws do not disappear because a property is sold "as-is," and insurance companies can void coverage for undisclosed or unresolved hazards.

The negotiation shifted overnight. The final agreement included a $10,000 credit earmarked for electrical upgrades plus updated disclosures documenting the condition and the buyers' planned remediation.

In a single negotiation, a "small" electrical finding became a structured solution instead of a future dispute. Both sides walked away protected—the buyers financially and physically, the seller legally.

Why Safety Negotiations Protect Everyone

Safety issues create a completely different negotiation environment because, once documented, they transform from "deferred maintenance" into legally recognized defects with long-term implications for every future owner.

□ **RED FLAG #1:** "As-is" clauses do not eliminate disclosure obligations. Sellers must still disclose all known, material defects—safety hazards meet all three criteria under state disclosure laws.

When an inspection identifies aluminum wiring, an unsafe chimney, or missing egress windows, the seller is no longer deciding whether to complete a buyer's requested upgrade. They are deciding whether to take on permanent disclosure responsibilities, future insurance complications, and potential legal exposure.

Under state disclosure laws such as Florida's *Johnson v. Davis* standard, New York's Section 462, and Colorado's strict-duty rules, sellers must disclose all known, material, and latent defects. Safety hazards meet all three criteria.

Aluminum wiring is 55 times more likely to fail than copper wiring—documented by the CPSC as a fire hazard affecting over 2 million homes built between 1965 and 1975.

Non-disclosure can create significant legal consequences. Recent real cases show this clearly: a seller who failed to disclose prior roof damage resulted in a buyer receiving a $2,200 credit after the insurer increased premiums, while undisclosed knob-and-tube wiring in another case caused a complete insurance claim denial—even for damage unrelated to the wiring.

□ **ACTION STEP 1:** List every safety issue from your inspection report under three categories: electrical, structural, and fire/code hazards.

Once an inspector documents a safety hazard, that information must be disclosed to the next buyer if you walk away, meaning the issue becomes the seller's permanent responsibility.

Safety issues also activate two powerful gatekeepers: insurance companies and mortgage lenders. Both require homes to meet minimum safety thresholds before issuing policies or approving loans.

Insurance carriers frequently decline coverage for pre-1972 aluminum wiring, active knob-and-tube wiring, ungrounded outlets, failing chimneys, or inadequate electrical panels. If insurable at all, premiums can be two to three times higher than standard rates.

Lenders follow a similar pattern. FHA and many conventional lenders require full replacement of knob-and-tube before closing, mandate correction of electrical service below 100 amps, and require egress windows for basement bedrooms.

> Safety negotiations aren't about buyer preferences—they're about meeting mandatory lender and insurance requirements that determine whether the transaction can proceed.

The cost realities behind these issues reinforce why safety negotiations are both rational and necessary.

Electrical hazards are among the most expensive to address. Aluminum wiring replacement averages $8,000–$15,000, while full knob-and-tube rewiring ranges from $12,000–$36,600 depending on home size. Panel upgrades from 60 amps to modern 200-amp service range from $1,300–$2,000.

Structural repairs show even wider ranges: minor foundation cracks may cost $1,000–$3,000, but major stabilization or underpinning can reach $15,000–$30,000+.

> ☐ **ACTION STEP 2:** Within 7–10 days of inspection, get itemized estimates from two to three licensed contractors for each safety issue. Include materials, labor, permits, and code requirements.

Fire-related safety requirements also carry clear costs. Chimney repairs range from $160–$750 for minor issues, but full replacement can cost $10,000–$15,000. Egress windows, often required for code compliance, cost $2,500–$6,000+ for basement installations. Even smoke and carbon monoxide detector compliance can add $100–$200 per location installed.

These costs exist regardless of who buys the property, which is why documented safety issues consistently result in buyers negotiating 70–90% of repair costs as credits.

How to Negotiate Safety Issues

Negotiating safety issues starts with a clear cost assessment using real contractor numbers, not guesses.

Begin by listing each category of hazard from your inspection: electrical, structural, and fire/code items.

For electrical, use licensed electricians to price aluminum wiring replacement ($8,000–$15,000), knob-and-tube rewiring ($12,000–$36,600), panel upgrades ($1,300–$2,000), and any grounding or GFCI/AFCI work, which often adds another $1,000–$3,000.

> □ **RED FLAG #2:** Insurance companies can deny ANY claim—not just defect-related claims—if they discover undisclosed safety hazards after a policy is issued. Complete policy voids have occurred for undisclosed knob-and-tube wiring even when roof damage was unrelated.

Structural safety items come next: minor foundation stabilization may run $1,000–$5,000, while major underpinning or tiebacks can cost $15,000–$30,000+. Support beam corrections often fall in the $3,000–$20,000 range, and roof structural repairs another $3,000–$8,000+.

Fire and egress hazards must be priced as well: chimney repairs can be $160–$750 for small issues but up to $10,000–$15,000 for full replacement; chimney liners run $625–$7,000; egress windows typically cost $2,500–$6,000+ in basements and $3,500–$4,000 for bedrooms.

> □ **ACTION STEP 3:** Contact your insurance company and lender to confirm written coverage requirements and safety mandates. Compile all documentation into one organized packet.

Finally, add code items such as deck and stair rail compliance ($1,500–$4,000) and required smoke and carbon monoxide detectors at $100–$200 per location.

When you total these categories, you often see a safety compliance figure between $20,000 and $50,000+. That final number becomes the backbone of your negotiation.

Most insurers decline coverage entirely for active knob-and-tube wiring. Those that offer policies demand full replacement within 30 days and charge pre-

miums two to three times higher than standard rates.

During week two of escrow, present your negotiation request as a liability-protection solution for both parties. Show the seller the inspection report, contractor quotes, insurance limitations, and lender requirements.

Emphasize that these items must now be disclosed to future buyers if the current deal falls through, increasing the seller's long-term responsibility.

□ **ACTION STEP 4:** Present your negotiation request with inspection reports, contractor quotes, insurance denial letters, and lender requirements. Frame this as protecting the seller's legal and financial interests.

Remind them that undisclosed safety defects can lead to insurance claim denials, lender withdrawal, or post-closing disputes. Offer multiple resolution options such as a seller credit, seller-completed work with permits, or an escrow holdback.

Framing the request as protecting the seller's legal and financial interests reduces tension and increases cooperation.

□ **ACTION STEP 5:** Once agreement is reached, document all terms in a contract amendment. If the seller performs repairs, require licensed contractors, proper permits, and final inspection approvals before closing.

When to Walk Away vs. Proceed

WALK AWAY IF: Key safety findings look like an accident report rather than a repair list. If the seller refuses to address documented hazards, you face multiple major issues at once (aluminum or knob-and-tube wiring plus foundation movement or chimney failure), or total safety work is likely to exceed $30,000–$40,000, your best leverage is leaving.

A flat denial from an insurance company, or a lender who will not approve the loan until high-risk items are corrected, is a bright red line. Without coverage and financing, there is no safe deal.

□ **RED FLAG #3:** If total safety work exceeds $30,000–$40,000 and the seller refuses to negotiate, walking away protects you from long-term financial and physical risk.

PROCEED WITH CAUTION IF: The seller will negotiate but not meet your full request, the hazards are clearly fixable with licensed work, and insurance and lender will accept repairs before or shortly after closing. In that case, set a safety budget cap, often $10,000–$20,000, confirm all work will be permitted and inspected, and stop if the numbers exceed your comfort zone.

The Reward: Protection and Peace of Mind

A successful safety negotiation delivers a triple benefit: immediate protection, long-term financial stability, and the confidence that the property is now insurable and financeable.

Aluminum Wiring Credit Protects Both Parties

One buyer faced active aluminum wiring in a 1970s home, a documented 55-times-higher fire hazard. Contractor quotes ranged from $10,000–$12,000 for full replacement, and the buyer's insurer refused coverage until remediation.

Using these facts, the buyer negotiated a $10,500 credit—enough to complete COPALUM repairs on critical kitchen circuits immediately and schedule full replacement later.

The seller benefited as well: resolving the issue through a documented credit protected them from future disclosure disputes and avoided re-listing with a known hazard.

The property moved from "uninsurable risk" to a home with a clear path to compliance. The total reward was substantial: enhanced safety, insurance approval, lender acceptance, and preserved marketability for both sides.

Most importantly, the buyer gained peace of mind knowing a hidden hazard had been responsibly addressed.

Buyers who document safety hazards with contractor quotes, insurance denials, and lender requirements consistently extract 70–90% of repair costs as credits.

Chapters 4 through 8 have shown how to negotiate risk at the property level—flood zones, fire exposure, earthquake retrofits, environmental hazards, and now electrical, structural, and fire safety issues.

Chapter 9 shifts your focus from fixing individual problems to strengthening your position in competitive markets. This is where your research becomes your advantage.

While other buyers compete emotionally and bid without understanding total risk, you will enter every negotiation with documented costs, insurance data, and lender requirements that give you leverage others overlook.

□ **ACTION STEP 6:** Set a clear decision deadline—usually by the end of week two or three of escrow—to avoid delays. If the seller declines to address critical hazards, be prepared to walk away.

Even in rising-price markets, safety findings, code requirements, and insurance constraints create objective negotiation power that does not disappear simply because demand is high.

You will learn how to position offers, justify price adjustments, and navigate competition using the same data you gathered in Chapters 4–8.

This book isn't about scaring you away from homes—it's about giving you the information to make decisions that are right for YOU.

Chapter 8 Key Takeaways

□ Safety issues transform into legal liabilities once documented—sellers face disclosure obligations, insurance complications, and potential lawsuits

□ Aluminum wiring is 55 times more likely to fail than copper (CPSC data), and most insurers refuse coverage or charge premiums two to three times higher

□ Knob-and-tube wiring is considered uninsurable by most carriers, and lenders require full replacement before funding

□ "As-is" clauses do not eliminate disclosure duties—sellers must still disclose all known material defects

□ Documented safety issues consistently result in buyers negotiating 70–90% of repair costs as credits

□ Insurance claim denials for undisclosed hazards can void entire policies, denying coverage for ANY claim, not just defect-related damage

□ Use liability protection framing to reduce seller resistance—show how addressing issues protects them from future legal and financial exposure

----

Chapter Resources
Feel free to skip ahead if you'd like to continue reading.

Chapter 9

Negotiating Market Position

By the time you arrive for the second showing, you can feel the competition in the air. Cars line the street, the agent's phone keeps buzzing, and the words "We already have multiple offers" hang over every conversation.

The property ticks all the emotional boxes—great schools, updated kitchen, perfect backyard. It also sits in a flood zone, has a 20-year-old roof, and an outdated electrical system the inspector quietly flagged as "needing upgrade." Most buyers never connect those dots. They walk through, fall in love, and write offers at list price or higher, hoping enthusiasm will beat the crowd.

You do something different.

Instead of matching the emotional offers, you submit an offer $15,000 below list, paired with a three-page risk analysis. Page one: 30-year flood insurance cost projected at $42,000 based on real quotes. Page two: roof replacement required in three to five years at approximately $18,000. Page three: electrical upgrade estimated at $8,000 to correct safety issues and bring the panel to modern standards.

Total documented cost: $68,000.

While other buyers promise more money and fewer contingencies, your package offers something sellers value even more in 2025: certainty. Your analysis shows the home is still worth buying—but only at a price that accounts for real, long-term costs. It signals you are serious, qualified, and unlikely to renegotiate or walk away when inspections arrive, because you have already priced the risks in.

> □ **RED FLAG #1:** In markets where 15% of contracts fail, emotional buyers who skip risk research frequently back out during inspection—leaving sellers frustrated and relisting properties.

In a market where contracts collapse at record rates, that level of clarity feels priceless to sellers everywhere.

After reviewing every offer, the seller turns down higher prices and chooses yours: **$12,000 below list plus an $8,000 electrical credit at closing.**

You did not "win the bidding war" by outspending anyone. You won by showing the numbers first.

The Competitive Market Trap

Most buyers enter competitive markets believing the highest price wins. In reality, emotional bidding causes buyers to ignore property-specific risks entirely.

When multiple offers are expected, buyers react from fear rather than evaluating true ownership costs. They waive contingencies, shorten timelines, and agree to terms they have not considered.

This explains why **15.1% of pending home sales fell through in August 2025**—the highest August rate ever recorded. National data shows 70% of cancellations tied to inspection issues and 45% from financing problems.

Emotional bidding may win the first round, but it often causes frustration, regret, and costly escrow failures.

□ **ACTION STEP 1:** Before making any offer, calculate the total 30-year cost of ownership including insurance, deferred maintenance, and required upgrades.

The "winning" buyer begins due diligence and gets surprised by issues they never accounted for. Flood insurance quotes can be eye-opening—especially in Florida where wind policyholders must carry flood coverage by 2027. The 26% chance of flooding over 30 years becomes significant. In high-risk zones, premiums can be much higher.

□ **RED FLAG #2:** Buyers who skip insurance research immediately question their offer once they receive actual quotes during escrow.

Wildfire areas present similar issues—carriers have exited many zones entirely. Without insurance, no mortgage is possible.

Inspections create more complications. Nearly 36% of deals collapse at the inspection stage due to repair disagreements or unexpected costs. Buyers request extensive credits after already negotiating price concessions—sometimes prompting sellers to move on. The emotional buyer's "win" becomes a stressful renegotiation.

Your approach is completely different. You identify risks upfront. You know insurance costs, flood implications, mitigation expenses, and financing barriers tied to aging systems.

While others submit offers based on list price and neighborhood appeal, your offer reflects documented expenses and long-term ownership realities.

You become the highest-certainty buyer, even if not the highest-price buyer. Sellers value certainty—41% of sales fell through recently, and risk-affected homes sit longer (Florida's 53 days versus national 45 days).

Your competitive advantage is knowing what others will discover too late.

The Market Position Formula

The market position formula begins with a simple principle: **competitive markets reward clarity, not emotion.**

While buyers race to submit offers based on fear, you calculate your maximum using documented costs.

Identify every risk-related expense. A high-risk flood zone may require $42,000 in 30-year insurance costs. An aging roof needs $18,000 replacement in three to five years. Outdated electrical panels require $8,000 in upgrades. **Total: $68,000.**

□ **ACTION STEP 2:** Create a simple formula: List Price - Documented Risk Costs = Your Maximum Data-Backed Offer.

Next, compare to similar properties without these risks. If low-risk properties sell for $475,000 while the target lists at $510,000, the gap becomes your negotiation point.

Your rational maximum: $510,000 list minus $68,000 documented costs = **$442,000.** Emotional buyers may offer $515,000 because competition feels intense. You anchor to reality.

The formula is straightforward: List Price minus Documented Costs equals Your Maximum Data-Backed Offer.

Research shows wildfire zones trade at 4% discounts, while flood zones discount 4.7% to 10.6%. Sellers respect offers grounded in financial logic.

You present a package: flood maps showing FEMA classifications, insurance quotes from licensed carriers, contractor estimates, and comparable sales adjusted for risk. The seller sees you have done serious homework, understand real costs, and will not renegotiate later.

□ **ACTION STEP 3:** Gather contractor estimates for any visible deferred maintenance (roof, electrical, HVAC) before making your offer.

When other buyers offer $515,000 with no risk analysis, sellers know there is a strong chance those buyers will request $20,000 in credits after inspection. Your $442,000 offer backed by documentation feels safer.

Sellers choose certainty over speculation, especially when 15% of contracts are failing nationwide.

Warning Signs: When to Walk Away

□ **RED FLAG #3:** If the seller refuses to review your documented risk analysis, they are hoping to sell to an uninformed buyer who will discover issues later.

Walk away if your data-backed maximum is exceeded by more than 4-10% above comparable properties. Buyers typically pay 101-104% of list during peak months—anything beyond reflects emotional bidding, not market value.

Walk away if the seller refuses to engage with your risk analysis or ignores documented costs. This signals bad-faith negotiation.

Walk away if pressure tempts you to waive critical contingencies. No competitive advantage is worth buying a home with unknown problems.

□ **RED FLAG #4:** Waiving inspection contingencies may feel strategic, but 70% of failed deals involve inspection disputes—you are gambling with your largest investment.

Proceed with caution if you are near your maximum and the gap is within a few percentage points. Sometimes small adjustments are acceptable if location or long-term potential justifies it.

□ **ACTION STEP 4:** Write your walk-away number on paper before negotiations and commit to honoring it regardless of competition.

The Step-by-Step Execution Plan

Step 1: Complete All Risk Research Before Offering

Complete every category of risk analysis before thinking about price. Review FEMA flood maps, wildfire data, wind exposure, environmental proximity, and safety concerns. Gather homeowners and flood insurance quotes. Obtain contractor estimates for roofs, electrical panels, plumbing, and structural items.

□ **ACTION STEP 5:** Get contractor estimates for all visible maintenance issues before the property hits the market if possible.

Step 2: Calculate Data-Backed Maximum

Subtract documented risks from the list price or comparable low-risk homes. This establishes your ceiling. Put your walk-away number in writing and commit to it regardless of competition.

Your advantage is clarity: you know the true cost of ownership over time while emotional buyers only see the list price.

Step 3: Prepare Comprehensive Analysis Package

Create a clean package with flood/fire/climate analysis, inspection findings, insurance quotes, and contractor estimates. Add comparable sales with risk adjustments (high-risk properties sell for 4-10% less and stay on market longer). Include an executive summary.

☐ **ACTION STEP 6:** Create a one-page executive summary highlighting documented costs and your offer rationale.

Step 4: Position Offer Strategically

State that your offer already accounts for all known risks, insurance requirements, and repairs—which means you will not renegotiate during escrow. Attach your analysis packet. Offer a quick closing with strong pre-approval.

Sellers prioritize reliability over the highest price, especially when nearly half of all deals are failing due to financing and inspection issues.

Step 5: Maintain Discipline During Negotiation

Stay grounded in your maximum. Do not increase based on pressure or emotion. Remind sellers that high offers often fall apart during inspection or insurance underwriting. Be willing to walk away.

☐ **ACTION STEP 7:** Reiterate that your offer eliminates renegotiation risk because all costs are already documented and priced in.

☐ **ACTION STEP 8:** If the seller counters above your maximum, politely restate your position and be prepared to walk away immediately.

The Proof: Certainty Beats Emotion

A Minneapolis buyer faced 37 showings in two days and 18 offers—including escalation clauses, waived inspections, and appraisal gap guarantees. Instead of joining the emotional surge, the buyer submitted a full analysis packet: comparable sales, pre-inspection findings ($15,000 in repairs), and insurance quotes.

While others bid $50,000+ over list, this buyer offered slightly below list with verifiable due diligence.

The Result: The seller—exhausted by collapsed offers—accepted. The buyer secured the home $12,000 below list and received an $8,000 credit. **Total savings: $20,000+** by presenting certainty over emotion.

Sellers choose the buyer they trust to close, not necessarily the buyer who offers the most money.

This proves a critical principle: **sellers choose the buyer they trust to close.** When contracts fail at historic rates and inspection disputes derail deals, certainty becomes more valuable than speculation.

Your competitive advantage is not outbidding the market—it is out-preparing it. You show up with documentation and discipline while others show up with emotion and hope. The result: you negotiate from strength, secure fair value, and avoid costly mistakes.

Chapter 9 Key Takeaways

□ Competitive markets reward clarity and certainty, not emotional bidding

□ 15.1% of pending sales fell through in August 2025—highest August rate ever recorded

□ 70% of failed deals involve inspection/repair disputes; 45% fail due to financing problems

□ The market position formula: List Price - Documented Costs = Maximum Data-Backed Offer

□ Risk properties (flood, fire, climate) sell for 4-10% less and sit on market 8+ days longer

□ Complete all risk research BEFORE making offers—flood insurance, contractor estimates, comparable sales

□ Create comprehensive analysis packages that demonstrate certainty of closing

□ Position your offer strategically by emphasizing that all costs are already priced in

□ Maintain discipline during negotiation—never exceed your data-backed maximum

□ Walk away if sellers refuse to acknowledge documented risks or pressure you to waive critical contingencies

□ Real example: Minneapolis buyer saved $20,000+ by submitting data-driven offer in 18-offer competition

□ Sellers value buyers who won't renegotiate later over buyers who promise the highest price upfront

Winning in competitive markets is not about outbidding others—it is about out-preparing them. Property-specific risks give you negotiating leverage because they reveal long-term costs many buyers miss.

But your next advantage is even stronger: regulatory issues. While flood exposure and climate risk influence value, regulatory problems create legal requirements that shape the entire transaction. Unpermitted additions, zoning conflicts, incomplete renovations, missing certificates, and code violations are not optional.

Regulatory compliance problems transform into powerful negotiation tools that reduce price, create credits, or require the seller to complete repairs before closing.

Lenders, appraisers, and insurers require corrections before closing. Sellers cannot dismiss these through preference or emotion. This transforms compliance problems into powerful negotiation tools.

Chapter 10 shows you how to identify these issues, verify them using public records, and turn regulatory obligations into clear negotiation gains.

Chapter Resources

Feel free to skip ahead if you'd like to continue reading.

Market negotiation demands competitive intelligence. Understanding your leverage requires understanding market context—days on market, comparable sales, neighborhood trends, and risk factors that affect demand. Visit **HomeDataReports.com** to generate reports combining property risk data with market intelligence. Our risk calculator shows you immediately if properties carry risks that explain extended listing times or price reductions. Create your free account and get your first Essential report revealing risks that might be suppressing buyer interest and creating negotiation opportunity.

Install the Chrome extension to research market position while browsing listings—properties with 90+ days on market plus flood zones or environmental concerns signal negotiation leverage. Tell your realtor about our partner program—agents who join can provide risk-adjusted market analysis to clients, explaining why some properties linger while others sell fast. The digital toolkit includes market positioning worksheets. When you understand WHY a property sits unsold, you negotiate from knowledge instead of guessing.

Chapter 10

Negotiating Regulatory Issues—Unpermitted Work, Zoning Violations, and Code Compliance

The lender was the first one to notice it. Halfway through underwriting, the appraiser's report hit their desk: tax records showed 1,600 square feet, but the photos and floor plan clearly showed a fourth bedroom and extra bathroom. The numbers did not match, and the note at the bottom was brief but decisive: "Unpermitted addition suspected. Confirm permits or treat as non-living area."

Overnight, the bonus suite in the back of the house stopped being a selling feature and became a financing condition. The lender's position was non-negotiable: either the seller obtained retroactive permits and engineering sign-off before closing, or the loan would be approved only on the original 1,600 permitted square feet—with a lower value and a larger cash requirement from the buyer.

When the listing agent called the building department, the answer confirmed what county records already showed: no permits on file. A retroactive permit package would require plans, engineering, and multiple inspections. After-the-fact permits alone typically cost $2,000–$8,000, while full legalization projects with upgrades and penalties often run $25,000–$45,000 or more. In this case, the contractor's estimate for permitting and corrections came back at $8,000–$12,000, with a clear warning that non-compliant work could be ordered partially demolished if it failed inspection.

The lender's file notes read like a checklist of demands, not suggestions, with completion dates that control your closing.

The seller's first reaction was familiar: "Everyone around here has unpermitted space." The lender's stance did not change. Until permits were issued or the addition removed, the file would not move to "clear to close," and the buyer's timeline stayed on hold.

The buyer stayed calm and precise: permits before closing at the seller's expense, or a $15,000 price reduction plus written indemnity covering future code enforcement. The final agreement landed on seller-completed retroactive permits at a documented cost of $9,500, full reports and approvals provided at closing.

Here's how to use regulatory requirements as leverage.

Why lenders block unpermitted work

The first problem with unpermitted work is the **lender blockade**. Conventional lenders will not quietly ignore known regulatory violations. When an appraiser notes an unpermitted addition or a square footage mismatch, the appraisal often becomes "subject to" conditions: obtain retroactive permits, prove code compliance, or remove the unpermitted work before closing.

Fannie Mae guidelines allow value for non-permitted space only when there are at least three comparable sales showing market acceptance; otherwise, the space receives little or no value and the loan is underwritten only on the legal square footage. In many cases, lenders issue conditional approvals that do not fund until the violation is resolved.

> □ **RED FLAG #1:** Some lenders, and most government-backed loans like FHA and VA, simply decline properties with unpermitted structural, electrical, or plumbing work altogether.

In practical terms, the lender's file notes read like a checklist of demands, not suggestions, with completion dates that control your closing. At that point, your "dream house" becomes a loan file with a stop sign on it. Until the regulatory issue is addressed, the transaction cannot move forward.

> Lenders treat unpermitted work as a financing condition, not a buyer preference—your timeline depends on resolution.

The second problem is the **liability time bomb**. Building and zoning codes generally do not have a true statute of limitations the way criminal or civil claims do. If unpermitted work is discovered in five, ten, or twenty years, the municipality can still require full compliance.

In many jurisdictions, ownership transfer itself is a trigger: the title search, survey, or certificate of occupancy review exposes old violations that must be addressed before the buyer can close or the seller can refinance. Once you own the property, any outstanding violations become your problem, not the previous owner's.

Retroactive permits usually start in the $2,000–$8,000 range just for fees and plan review, but full legalization projects often run $18,500–$45,000 for typical garage conversions.

If the work fails modern code, the local government can require partial or full demolition before approving new construction. The seller who did work without permits frequently used lower-cost materials or skipped inspections elsewhere, which means the visible issue is rarely the only concern.

□ **RED FLAG #2:** Complex additions with bathrooms or structural changes can exceed $45,000–$75,000 to bring into full compliance.

The third problem is that once unpermitted work is discovered, it becomes the **seller's ongoing challenge**. Disclosure laws and standard seller forms require owners to state whether they know of any code violations, open permits, or unpermitted work. After a failed inspection or conditional appraisal, a seller cannot legally "forget" the issue with the next buyer.

In New Jersey, a high-end sale collapsed when buyers discovered extensive unpermitted renovations and requested a six-figure price reduction; the seller refused, that deal failed, and a later sale was completely voided in court when the violations were concealed.

In Florida, standard FAR/BAR contracts give buyers the right to cancel if unpermitted work cannot be resolved within the agreed permit limit. Properties with persistent violations eventually migrate to a smaller pool of cash-only buyers willing to inherit the risk at a discount.

Regulatory issues create the strongest negotiation leverage because they block transactions.

The retroactive permitting cost structure

Negotiating regulatory issues begins with a **clear financial picture**. Retroactive permitting is not a single fee—it is a sequence of costs that accumulate as the building department evaluates the work.

Here's the typical cost structure:

Permit penalties and after-the-fact permit fees: \$2,000–\$8,000 (California averages \$500–\$2,000 for less complex situations)

Architectural or engineering plans: \$2,000–\$4,000, or 5–20% of total project costs

Structural engineering reviews: \$1,500–\$3,500

Code upgrades (electrical, plumbing, HVAC): \$2,000–\$10,000 depending on deficiencies

Inspections: \$100–\$500 per inspection, with multiple inspections required throughout the retroactive process

Garage conversions or bedroom additions: \$18,500–\$45,000 total

Complex additions with bathrooms or structural changes: \$45,000–\$75,000+

Potential fines: \$250–\$1,000 per day for continuing violations, escalating further for repeat issues

□ **ACTION STEP 1:** Request official permit search from the building department within the first 3 days of escrow.

If the work does not meet current standards, municipalities can order partial or complete removal, which can add thousands more in demolition and rebuild costs. When these categories are combined—after-the-fact permits, professional plans, inspections, penalties, upgrades, and possible removal—the total regulatory risk often ranges from \$10,000 on the low end to \$50,000 or more for complex cases.

Presenting this cost structure as a single quantified assessment gives you a strong factual basis for negotiation.

Documentation is the second part of the strategy. You begin by comparing county property records and permit histories with the actual structure. If square footage, bedroom count, or bathroom count differ from recorded data, you document the discrepancy with dated photos and a floor plan.

Next, check zoning compliance to identify setbacks, use-designation issues, and potential nonconforming elements. Then obtain an official search for open or expired permits and outstanding code violations.

□ **ACTION STEP 2:** Compare tax records to actual structure—photograph every discrepancy with dated images.

At the same time, request the lender's policy on unpermitted work in writing—most lenders require full legalization or exclusion of the unpermitted area from valuation, which affects financing eligibility. Finally, secure written contractor estimates for retroactive permits and required upgrades.

Each piece of documentation serves a specific role: it establishes the facts, demonstrates lender constraints, quantifies costs, and highlights risk that future buyers will face as well.

Once the facts are established, you use **lender requirements as a communication tool**. The core script is: "Our lender requires this to be resolved before funding." This removes emotion and makes the request procedural rather than personal.

You then reinforce the structure: "This is not our preference—it is a transaction requirement. We cannot obtain financing until the unpermitted work is either legalized or removed."

□ **ACTION STEP 3:** Obtain written lender policy stating resolution requirements—use this as negotiation anchor.

From there, you present the options: "We have three paths. You obtain retroactive permits and provide proof before closing; or you provide a price reduction and an indemnity for future code enforcement; or you remove the unpermitted work and restore the property to permitted condition."

A second script emphasizes the financing consequence: "Without resolution, the property becomes a cash-only sale. No conventional, FHA, or VA lender will fund the unpermitted space without compliance documentation."

A third script draws from appraisal policy: "The appraiser cannot assign value to the non-permitted square footage without three comparable sales. The lender will underwrite only the permitted square footage unless permits are obtained."

These statements anchor the negotiation in regulatory and lending realities.

When to walk away vs. proceed with caution

Walk away if the seller will not address the unpermitted work or refuses all solutions required by the lender. Retroactive permitting becomes impractical when estimated costs exceed $20,000–$30,000, especially for complex additions involving plumbing, structural changes, or garage conversions that may require $45,000–$75,000 in full legalization.

□ **RED FLAG #3:** If engineering reviews suggest a meaningful risk of partial demolition, the long-term liability outweighs the potential value.

You should also exit the transaction if the lender declines all proposed resolutions or if multiple unpermitted elements increase the overall compliance burden. When the lender, building department, and contractor findings all point toward high regulatory risk, the safest strategy is to move on.

Proceed with caution if the seller agrees to obtain permits, fund escrow, or provide a substantial credit plus indemnity. Straightforward unpermitted work with a clear permitting path may be acceptable if the property's value justifies the effort. Ensure indemnity language protects against future enforcement and calculate the maximum regulatory cost you are willing to absorb.

□ **RED FLAG #4:** Properties with persistent violations eventually migrate to a smaller pool of cash-only buyers willing to inherit the risk at a discount.

5-step regulatory compliance checklist

Step 1: Order permit search immediately

Request an official permit search from your local building department during the first 3 days of escrow. Provide the property address and parcel number. Most jurisdictions charge $50–$150 for a comprehensive permit history, which lists all open permits, closed permits, violations, and stop-work orders. Cross-reference the results against the property's current condition—focus on square footage, bedroom count, bathroom count, and major structural changes. Flag any discrepancies between recorded permits and actual construction.

□ **ACTION STEP 4:** Order permit search within 3 days—cost $50–$150, cross-reference against current structure.

Step 2: Verify zoning compliance

Check the property's zoning designation and confirm that all structures comply with setback, height, and use restrictions. Many municipalities provide zoning maps and code requirements online, but for complex properties, request a zoning compliance letter directly from the planning department. Document any nonconforming uses or structures that predate current zoning, as these may require special permits or grandfathered status verification. Identify potential zoning violations such as commercial use in residential zones, accessory dwelling unit restrictions, or density violations.

Step 3: Obtain contractor cost estimates

Hire a licensed contractor to evaluate the unpermitted work and provide a written estimate for obtaining retroactive permits. The estimate should include after-the-fact permit fees, architectural or engineering plan costs, structural reviews if applicable, code upgrade expenses for electrical, plumbing, or HVAC systems, and inspection fees. Request itemized pricing and a timeline estimate showing how long the permitting process will take. Ensure the contractor includes potential penalties and the cost of bringing work up to current code, creating a clear financial map of what compliance will require.

□ **ACTION STEP 5:** Obtain written contractor estimate breaking down all permit, engineering, and upgrade costs.

Step 4: Present lender requirement

Now assemble your findings into a concise negotiation packet. Frame the issue as a transaction requirement, not a buyer preference. Lead with the written lender policy stating that the unpermitted work must be resolved before funding. Add contractor estimates, permit fee ranges, and the projected timeline.

Next, present resolution options: seller obtains permits before closing, seller provides a price reduction plus indemnity, seller funds an escrow for permitting based on 120–200% of estimated cost, or seller removes the unpermitted work. Provide these options during week 1–2 of escrow, giving the seller time to evaluate but making it clear that the lender's conditions must be met.

□ **ACTION STEP 6:** Present resolution options in weeks 1–2 with written lender policy as negotiation anchor.

Step 5: Formalize resolution

Once an agreement is reached, document the terms in a written contract amendment. If the seller will obtain permits, outline the required work, deadline extensions, and the documentation needed before closing—such as finalized permits, inspection approvals, and contractor certifications.

If the seller is providing a credit and indemnity, include a detailed indemnification clause protecting the buyer from future code enforcement actions. If escrow funding is used, specify deposit amount, release conditions, and oversight requirements. Finally, set a firm walk-away deadline if compliance cannot be guaranteed. Complete this during week 2 of escrow, ensuring all parties understand responsibilities before proceeding to closing.

□ **ACTION STEP 7:** Formalize resolution in written amendment—include deadlines, documentation requirements, and walk-away dates.

A fully financeable property with zero future liability

The outcome of effective regulatory negotiation is clarity, protection, and a fully financeable property.

A buyer discovered an unpermitted bedroom and bathroom addition that triggered an appraisal hold. The lender required retroactive permits or removal before approving the loan. Instead of accepting the risk, the buyer used lender requirements and documented costs to negotiate a firm resolution. The seller obtained retroactive permits at a verified cost of $9,500, including engineering review and updated inspections. Once the permits were finalized, the lender reclassified the space as legal living area, allowing the property to appraise at full value. The buyer avoided $10,000–$20,000 in potential liability exposure and eliminated the chance of future enforcement actions or costly demolition. Most importantly, the home became fully financeable now and more marketable for resale later.

The regulatory issue that once blocked the transaction became a documented strength.

This brings us to the transition into Part 3. In Part 2, you learned how to negotiate every major risk category using data instead of emotion. Chapters 4 through 10 walked you through flood risk, fire exposure, earthquake safety, environmental contamination, property safety hazards, market positioning, and regulatory compliance. You now understand how each category creates leverage, how to quantify the costs, and how to convert those numbers into stronger negotiation outcomes. With these tools, you can evaluate any property with confidence.

Part 3 shifts from analysis to execution. Now that you know how to evaluate risk and negotiate each category, the next section shows you how to put everything together—from the 48-hour due diligence blitz, to presenting findings, to closing the deal with precision.

You've learned the strategies. Now it's time to use them. The next section transforms these negotiations into real results.

Chapter 10 Key Takeaways

□ Lenders treat unpermitted work as a financing condition—your timeline depends on resolution, not seller cooperation.

□ Retroactive permit costs range from $2,000–$8,000 for basic work to $45,000–$75,000+ for complex additions with structural changes.

□ Building codes generally have no statute of limitations—violations discovered decades later still require compliance.

□ Use lender requirements as leverage: "Our lender requires this resolved before funding."

□ Document the gap between tax records and actual structure with photos, permit searches, and contractor estimates.

□ Present three options: seller obtains permits, seller provides reduction plus indemnity, or seller removes unpermitted work.

□ Walk away when estimated costs exceed $20,000–$30,000 or engineering reviews suggest demolition risk.

Chapter Resources

Feel free to skip ahead if you'd like to continue reading.

Regulatory negotiation requires verification. Before you negotiate unpermitted work or code violations, you need documentation beyond the seller's disclosure form. Generate comprehensive property reports at **HomeDataReports.com** that include permit history, zoning verification, and compliance records where available through public databases. Our risk calculator flags properties in areas with strict code enforcement or zoning changes affecting use. Create your account and get your first Essential report free—revealing the regulatory context that affects property value and financing.

Download the Chrome extension to research regulatory concerns while browsing properties. Share this with your real estate attorney and home inspector—when they join our partner referral network, they can access property intelligence that reveals potential regulatory issues before clients make offers. The video masterclass covers real examples of buyers negotiating unpermitted work using documented evidence. The digital toolkit includes code compliance checklists. Regulatory leverage comes from verifiable facts, not assumptions.

Chapter 11

The 48-Hour Due Diligence Blitz

Friday at 3:17 p.m., your offer is accepted and the clock starts. Earnest money is wired by 4:30. Before most buyers have finished texting family, you and your agent are moving.

Saturday, 8:05 a.m.: the inspection is booked for the earliest slot the next morning. By 8:30, you have flood, fire, seismic, and environmental data pulled from federal databases and your risk report saved as a single PDF. By noon, three insurance quotes are in your inbox, showing premiums nearly two thousand dollars higher per year than comparable low-risk homes.

Saturday afternoon, you tag the major risks and start building your list. Old roof. Tired HVAC. Electrical panel at capacity. While other buyers are enjoying their weekend, you are drafting emails to three roofing contractors, two HVAC companies, and one electrician with photos attached and "24-hour quote requested" in the subject line.

Sunday, 9:00 a.m.: the inspection begins. By 11:30, the inspector has confirmed what the databases hinted at—roof near end-of-life, aging HVAC, dated electrical. At 3:45 p.m., the full digital report hits your inbox. By early evening, contractor estimates arrive showing total documented cost exceeding twenty-eight thousand dollars.

Monday, 8:59 a.m.—Hour 72. Your agent delivers a clean, three-part package: inspection excerpts, contractor quotes, and a one-page summary requesting a price reduction plus credits at closing, tied directly to the documented repairs. The seller resists, then calls their own contractor, who lands in the same cost range.

By Monday afternoon, you have a signed addendum: twenty thousand dollars off the price and five thousand in credits. While competing buyers are still trying to get on an inspector's calendar, you have already turned 48 hours of focused due diligence into twenty-five thousand dollars of real, written concessions. This is the 48-hour edge.

The first 48 hours decide whether the inspection window works for you—or against you.

Why Most Buyers Waste Their Best Window

Most buyers waste the most valuable part of the deal: the first 48 hours after their offer is accepted. They feel relief, they are tired, and they think, "We have a 7–10 day inspection window. There's plenty of time." So they wait. They schedule the inspection for "later next week." They tell themselves they will "look into" insurance and risk data once the report comes in.

By the time they finally act, the clock has turned against them.

Here is what the data shows. When buyers present a complete negotiation package early—within three to five days of the inspection report—sellers agree to reasonable repair requests about sixty to seventy-five percent of the time. When buyers wait until the end of the contingency window, acceptance drops below forty percent.

> Buyers who present comprehensive documentation early see sixty to seventy-five percent acceptance rates on reasonable requests versus under forty percent for late submissions.

Timing is not the only problem. Credibility is the second hit. A buyer who says, "I think the roof needs work" gets brushed aside. A buyer who shows an inspection excerpt plus three contractor quotes for a specific roof replacement is much harder to ignore. Research shows sellers respond very differently based on documentation quality:

- Inspection report only: thirty to forty percent negotiate meaningfully
- Report plus one estimate: fifty to sixty percent
- Report plus two or three estimates: sixty-five to eighty percent
- Report plus multiple estimates plus engineer letter: seventy-five to eighty-five percent

Most buyers never get past the first level. They ask for repairs without real numbers. Sellers know this, and they use it. They say, "We do not agree. The home has been fine for years." Without documentation, the conversation ends there.

Then comes leverage loss. By day eight to ten, the seller knows the buyer is emotionally attached. The buyer has mentally moved in. Friends know the address. The family has planned the furniture layout. At that point, a "take it or leave it" stance works in the seller's favor. Late requests feel like pressure, not like due diligence. Many sellers simply refuse to negotiate.

□ **RED FLAG #1:** Waiting until day nine or ten to submit repair requests triggers seller skepticism. Acceptance rates drop by more than half compared to early presentation.

The cost of this disorder is real. Nationally, four to seven percent of contracts terminate and about sixteen percent are delayed, often because contingencies were not handled well. Earnest money disputes now show up in an estimated eight to twelve percent of deals. On a five-hundred-thousand-dollar home with fifteen thousand in earnest money, a missed inspection deadline can mean losing the entire deposit and still facing defects that cost thirty thousand or more to fix.

Data becomes leverage, leverage becomes concessions, and concessions protect your budget.

The Complete Timeline

The 48-hour blitz is a checklist on a clock. You are not "kind of" doing due diligence. You are running a clear system with time blocks and specific tasks.

Hours 0–4: Contract Execution and Setup

As soon as the offer is accepted, the timer starts. Sign the purchase contract, deliver earnest money immediately, and confirm in writing that all inspection and due diligence contingencies are active with clear deadlines and exact dates.

Request every seller document immediately. In the same email, ask for title report, survey, HOA documents, seller disclosures, receipts for major repairs, current insurance declaration page, and the last two to three years of property tax bills.

Schedule the inspection within two to four hours. Contact your inspector as soon as the contract is signed. Target the earliest morning slot, ideally the next morning. Professional inspectors deliver reports within twenty-four to forty-eight hours.

□ **ACTION STEP 1:** Book inspection within four hours of contract acceptance. Morning slots get priority and maximize report timing.

Create a digital folder: [Property Address] – Due Diligence. Inside it, add subfolders for Contract & Deadlines, Seller Docs, Inspection & Tests, Federal Databases, Insurance Quotes, Contractor Quotes, and Negotiation Package.

Hours 4–12: Database Research Blitz

While you wait for the inspection, run federal risk databases in this order. Total time: fifteen to twenty-five minutes without aggregation tools.

FEMA flood maps take one to two minutes. EPA EnviroFacts returns environmental contamination records in seconds. USGS provides geological and seismic data immediately. NOAA coastal and climate data queries execute in seconds to minutes. Census APIs provide demographic and neighborhood data in seconds.

Aggregation services like Smarty distill four hundred sixty-five-plus data points across eighteen natural hazards in under two minutes versus fifteen to twenty-five minutes of manual lookups.

For each risk source, take a screenshot, save it with a clear file name, and note clear red flags: flood zone A or AE, near Superfund site, high seismic zone, severe wildfire or wind risk. You are not negotiating yet. You are building the evidence file.

Hours 12–24: Inspection and Professional Inputs

Attend the inspection in person. The inspection is where you collect most of your leverage. Walk the property with the inspector. Ask them to rank findings: safety or code, major systems, cosmetic. Take your own photos of anything they flag. Ask which items usually cost over one thousand dollars to fix.

> □ **ACTION STEP 2:** Attend inspection in person. Take photos and notes on every safety, structural, and major system issue.

Order add-on tests based on what you saw. Common add-ons include radon test, sewer scope for older homes, chimney inspection if wood-burning, roof certification if roof is ten-plus years old, and mold or moisture checks if there is past water damage.

Request insurance quotes. Send a simple packet to three to five carriers or brokers and request standard homeowners, flood if in or near a flood zone, and wind or hurricane or earthquake if relevant. Ask for annual premium, deductibles, and any coverage exclusions tied to the home's condition.

Hours 24–36: Contractor Quote Collection

The minute the inspection report arrives, move on contractor quotes. Reach out to at least two contractors per major category from your inspection report. For each contractor, send property address, specific issue description from inspection, relevant photos, inspection excerpt if helpful, and requested response time: twenty-four to forty-eight hours.

Use contractors who offer remote quotes based on photos and descriptions when feasible. Many roofers can estimate from photos and satellite imagery. HVAC companies can quote based on model numbers and photos. Electricians can estimate panel upgrades from panel photos and load calculations.

□ **ACTION STEP 3:** Contact contractors within twelve hours of report arrival. Attach photos and inspection excerpts with each quote request.

Group issues into three tiers. Tier 1 Critical: safety, code violations, structural issues, and systems at end of life. Tier 2 Significant: aging systems, efficiency concerns, insurance-impacting issues. Tier 3 Minor: cosmetic, normal maintenance, wish-list items. Focus your contractor outreach on Tier 1 and high-cost Tier 2 items.

Hours 36–48: Negotiation Package Assembly

Now you turn raw data into a clear, simple offer. Draft a one-page executive summary. Include total documented costs with range, Tier 1, 2, and 3 totals, your proposed solution, and requested response deadline.

Build the issue-by-issue analysis. For each Tier 1 and Tier 2 item, include problem description, documentation with inspection page reference and photo and contractor quote, cost with specific numbers, and impact on safety or insurance or lender or resale.

Multiple contractor quotes accomplish two objectives: price validation preventing inflated estimates, and seller confidence in repair assessments.

Assemble supporting documents. Attach, in this order: inspection report excerpts for key items, contractor estimates grouped by type, insurance quotes showing higher premiums if risk is not fixed, and federal database screenshots for flood, environmental, and seismic risk if relevant. Label everything clearly so the seller can follow the logic.

Present clear resolution options. Offer one to two clean paths: price reduction tied to documented costs, credit at closing, or seller completes specific repairs before closing with proof. Avoid vague "fix everything" language. Tie each request to a document and a dollar amount.

□ **ACTION STEP 4:** Send complete package by Hour 48 to maximize leverage while sellers are most receptive.

By Hour 48, you have a complete, documented negotiation package on the table—days before most buyers even finish scheduling their inspection.

Critical Warning Signs

□ **RED FLAG #2:** Seller delays providing requested documents within the first twenty-four to forty-eight hours. This can signal hidden issues or disorganization. Send a formal written request with a twenty-four-hour deadline.

□ **RED FLAG #3:** Inspection reveals significantly more issues than expected. Total repair costs may exceed your budget. Build a complete cost list and compare to your maximum budget. Walk away if critical issues exceed your financial capacity.

□ **RED FLAG #4:** You are rushing to meet the deadline without complete data. If you reach day seven to ten without contractor quotes, insurance data, or a complete issue list, request a three to five day contingency extension with a clear reason.

When to Walk, When to Fight

Risk tolerance is simple: match the issues to your budget and your comfort level. Walk away when total documented repairs exceed ten percent of the purchase price and push past what you can safely afford. Research shows major defects like foundation repairs or roof-plus-HVAC bundles often lead to failed deals when buyers try to force the numbers.

Cancel if safety or health issues appear and the seller refuses to address them, or if you cannot secure contractor quotes in time.

Proceed with confidence when every major item has clear estimates, the total cost fits your budget, and no Tier 1 safety risks remain. Buyers who present complete documentation early see sixty to seventy-five percent acceptance rates on reasonable requests.

Request a contingency extension when you need a structural engineer, environmental testing, or detailed quotes. Taking three to five extra days is better than rushing into a costly mistake.

Early Detection Wins: One buyer scheduled inspection within forty-eight hours, identified foundation concern, and hired structural engineer on Day 4. Engineer confirmed repair cost of thirty-eight to forty-two thousand dollars. Buyer presented report on Day 6. Seller offered forty-thousand-dollar price reduction on Day 7. Net savings: over thirty-nine thousand dollars after eight-hundred-dollar engineer fee.

The Results

The buyer who executes the full 48-hour system sees results most buyers never experience. In one documented case, the buyer started the blitz Friday afternoon and completed every step by Monday morning. By Hour 72, they had a complete package: inspection findings, federal database screenshots, three roofing quotes, two HVAC quotes, and insurance estimates showing premiums nearly two thousand dollars higher per year than comparable homes.

The seller resisted at first, but the buyer's documentation was too strong to dismiss. Three contractor quotes confirmed the same ranges. Insurance data showed real long-term cost impact. Everything was organized, time-stamped, and easy to verify. The seller realized that any new buyer would uncover the same issues.

Final outcome: a twenty-thousand-dollar price reduction plus five-thousand-dollar repair credits. Total concessions of twenty-five thousand dollars—roughly eighty-eight percent of the documented Tier 1 costs. By comparison, similar buyers who waited until day nine of the contingency window in the same market averaged less than half that amount because sellers were no longer motivated to negotiate.

The negotiated savings covered nearly all major repairs planned for the next three years. This is the practical payoff of acting fast.

The deal stayed on schedule. No extensions were needed. The buyer closed with full clarity on every system, every upcoming repair, and every risk. There were no surprises after moving in, no emergency expenses, and no strain on the family's budget.

But information alone does not win deals. The 48-hour blitz gives you the data. Chapter 12 shows you how to **build your negotiation strategy**—how to use seller motivation, market conditions, and your priorities to turn that data into a tactical plan that gets results.

Chapter 11 Key Takeaways

□ The first 48 hours after contract acceptance determine your negotiation leverage

□ Early presentation (days 1-5) achieves sixty to seventy-five percent seller acceptance versus under forty percent for late packages

□ Book inspection within four hours of acceptance for optimal timing

□ Run federal databases (FEMA, EPA, USGS, NOAA, Census) in fifteen to twenty-five minutes or use aggregation tools for under two minutes

□ Contact two to three contractors per category within twelve hours of inspection report

□ Build negotiation package by Hour 48 with inspection excerpts, contractor quotes, and federal data

□ Multiple contractor quotes provide price validation and credibility—sellers cannot dismiss corroborated findings

□ Document everything in writing and tie every request to specific dollar amounts

----

48-hour due diligence checklists. The video masterclass shows buyers researching properties in minutes using our platform. The audiobook reinforces the blitz framework while you're driving to showings. When the market moves fast, your research tools need to move faster.

Chapter 12

Building Your Negotiation Strategy

Emily and Nathan had the data. Their report from HomeDataReports.com showed the property was in FEMA flood zone AE. Annual insurance would run $3,200. The home inspection revealed a cracked foundation slab, aging HVAC system, and a roof with three years of life remaining.

The sellers were asking $385,000. Comparable sales supported that number. But repairs would cost $28,000 according to three contractor quotes.

Emily wanted to negotiate. Nathan wanted to walk away. They had no strategy, no framework, no clear decision point. So they did what most buyers do—they made an emotional counteroffer of $365,000, hoping the sellers would split the difference.

The sellers rejected it immediately and accepted another offer two days later.

Emily and Nathan lost the home because they confused hoping with planning.

Data without strategy is just expensive information.

The Problem: Most Buyers Confuse Tactics with Strategy

Here's what happens in 90% of negotiations. Buyers find issues during inspection. They panic. They make a counteroffer based on gut feeling. They hope the seller accepts. They have no backup plan if the seller refuses.

That's not negotiation. That's gambling.

Real negotiation requires three things most buyers skip: **clear priorities**, **defined positions**, and **seller motivation analysis**. Without these, you're reacting instead of controlling the conversation.

The data you've gathered—flood risk, environmental hazards, crime statistics, school ratings, climate projections—is worthless if you can't translate it into leverage. And leverage only works when you know exactly what you want, what you'll accept, and when you'll walk away.

> □ **RED FLAG #1:** If your negotiation strategy is "see what happens," you've already lost. Sellers with experienced agents will test your resolve immediately.

Most buyers make one of three fatal mistakes. First, they present every issue they found without prioritizing them. Sellers see a scattered list and assume the buyers are fishing for concessions. Second, they anchor their opening offer to emotions instead of data. Third, they negotiate without knowing the seller's timeline or motivation.

The result? Buyers who could have secured $15,000 in concessions walk away with $3,000. Or worse—they overpay because they didn't know when to stop negotiating and when to walk.

The Strategy Framework: Five Steps to Negotiation Control

Successful negotiation isn't about winning arguments. It's about building a system that protects your interests while keeping the deal alive. This framework works whether you're negotiating over $5,000 in repairs or $50,000 in structural issues.

Step 1: Categorize Every Issue by Impact

Break every problem you've identified into three tiers based on safety, cost, and longevity.

Tier 1 - Non-Negotiable (Safety & Structure): Foundation cracks, roof leaks, electrical code violations, flood zone mandatory repairs, severe mold, structural damage. These are walk-away items if not addressed.

Tier 2 - High Priority (Major Systems): HVAC replacement, water heater, plumbing issues, septic problems, windows, significant deferred maintenance. These affect your budget within 12-36 months.

Tier 3 - Lower Priority (Cosmetic & Convenience): Paint, landscaping, minor appliances, outdated fixtures. Nice to get, but not deal-breakers.

Your negotiation power comes from knowing which tier matters most to you. If you treat every issue equally, sellers won't take you seriously.

> □ **ACTION STEP 1:** Create a three-column spreadsheet with Tier 1, Tier 2, and Tier 3 categories. Assign every inspection finding and data issue to one tier.

Step 2: Calculate Total Impact in Dollars

Get three contractor quotes for every repair. Don't rely on inspector estimates—they're not binding. Contractors provide real numbers you can reference during negotiation.

Add ongoing costs to your calculations. If the property is in a flood zone, that's $3,200 per year in insurance. Over five years, that's $16,000. If the roof needs replacement in three years instead of ten, that's a $7,000 acceleration of expected costs.

Document everything. Your negotiation strength comes from data, not opinions.

Sellers respond to numbers, not feelings. Three contractor quotes beat one angry email.

Step 3: Analyze Seller Motivation and Market Position

Negotiation leverage shifts based on four factors: seller timeline, market conditions, days on market, and competing offers.

High seller motivation indicators: Property listed over 45 days, multiple price reductions, seller already purchased next home, estate sale, divorce, job relocation, pre-foreclosure.

Low seller motivation indicators: New listing, multiple offers, seller still living in home with no move deadline, strong market with low inventory.

The more motivated the seller, the more leverage you have. If they've dropped the price twice and moved out three months ago, they're bleeding money on two mortgages. That's your opening.

> Motivated sellers negotiate on price and repairs. Unmotivated sellers walk away from reasonable requests because they can afford to wait for the next buyer.

Step 4: Define Three Clear Positions

Never enter a negotiation with one number. You need three: your opening position, your fallback position, and your walk-away line.

Opening Position: This is your ideal outcome. Cover all Tier 1 items, most Tier 2 items, and a few Tier 3 items. Expect pushback. That's normal.

Fallback Position: This is your realistic target. Cover all Tier 1 items and most Tier 2 items. This is where most deals close.

Walk-Away Line: This is your hard boundary. All Tier 1 items must be addressed, or you terminate the contract. No exceptions.

The walk-away line is the most important position most buyers never define. Without it, you'll accept deals that compromise your safety or budget just to avoid losing the house.

☐ **ACTION STEP 2:** Write down your three positions in dollars before you contact the seller. Calculate exact amounts for each tier.

☐ **RED FLAG #2:** If you can't define your walk-away line, you're not ready to negotiate. Sellers will sense uncertainty and push for concessions you can't afford.

Step 5: Build Your Presentation Package

The best negotiators don't argue. They present evidence and let the data speak.

Your package should include: inspection report excerpts highlighting Tier 1 and Tier 2 items, all contractor quotes with line-item breakdowns, photos documenting issues, insurance quotes showing ongoing costs (flood zone, wind, earthquake if applicable), comparable sales data showing market adjustments for similar issues.

Never present this emotionally. Keep your language neutral and fact-based. The goal is to make it easy for the seller to say yes without feeling attacked.

The seller who feels cornered will reject even reasonable requests. The seller who sees documented evidence will negotiate.

Red Flags: Negotiation Traps That Kill Deals

Even with a solid strategy, certain behaviors guarantee failure.

Trap 1: Negotiating Before You Have Leverage

Some buyers try to negotiate repairs before the inspection period. This fails because you haven't documented anything yet. Wait until you have contractor quotes, inspection reports, and insurance data. Then present everything at once.

Trap 2: Making Demands Without Deadlines

If you send a list of demands with no response deadline, the seller controls the timeline. Set a 48-72 hour response window. This keeps negotiations moving and prevents sellers from dragging out the process while they shop for better offers.

□ **RED FLAG #3:** If the seller responds with vague promises like "we'll think about it" or "let's see what we can do," that's a stalling tactic. Require specific commitments with timelines.

Trap 3: Accepting Seller Credits Instead of Repairs

Many sellers offer to credit you at closing instead of fixing problems. This sounds convenient until you realize you're now responsible for managing contractors, dealing with delays, and covering cost overruns. Only accept credits if you're confident you can manage the repairs yourself.

Trap 4: Focusing on Price Instead of Total Cost

A seller who drops the price by $10,000 but refuses to fix a $15,000 foundation issue hasn't given you a deal. Calculate total ownership costs—purchase price, repairs, insurance, maintenance—before deciding if the negotiation succeeded.

□ **ACTION STEP 3:** Calculate total cost of ownership for your target property. Include purchase price plus all Tier 1 and Tier 2 repairs.

Action Plan: Execute Your Strategy

Here's the step-by-step process to turn your framework into results.

Day 1-3 (Inspection Period): Order home inspection, request contractor quotes for all major repairs, pull flood insurance quotes if in FEMA zone, document all findings with photos.

Day 4-5 (Strategy Session): Categorize issues into Tier 1, 2, and 3, calculate total repair costs, define your three positions (opening, fallback, walk-away), research seller motivation indicators, prepare presentation package.

Day 6 (Presentation): Submit formal request with inspection excerpts, contractor quotes, insurance data, and your opening position. Set 48-hour response deadline. Keep tone professional and fact-based.

Day 7-8 (Negotiation): Review seller's response. If they reject your opening position, move to fallback position. If they reject fallback, decide whether to walk based on your predetermined line.

Day 9-10 (Resolution): Finalize agreement in writing with specific repair descriptions or credit amounts. Update contract with negotiated terms. Confirm all parties sign amendment.

□ **ACTION STEP 4:** Create a negotiation timeline spreadsheet with each day's required tasks. This prevents deadline confusion.

Negotiation is not about who wins the argument. It's about who has the better system.

Risk Tolerance: Knowing When to Hold and When to Fold

Not every negotiation succeeds. Sometimes the seller refuses reasonable requests. Sometimes the numbers don't work even after concessions. Your job is to know when to walk away before emotion overrides logic.

Walk away if: All Tier 1 safety issues remain unaddressed, total repair costs exceed your financial reserves, seller refuses to provide documentation or permits for previous repairs, seller delays responses repeatedly without explanation, your walk-away line is crossed.

Stay in the deal if: All Tier 1 items are resolved, Tier 2 items are partially addressed or credited reasonably, total costs still align with your budget, seller negotiates in good faith with timely responses.

The biggest mistake buyers make is treating every negotiation like a battle they must win. Sometimes the best outcome is walking away from a property that doesn't meet your baseline requirements.

CASE STUDY: The $18,000 Concession

James and Maria found a $340,000 home with flood zone exposure and aging systems. Their report showed $26,800 in documented repairs: Tier 1 items (roof leak, electrical) totaled $12,500. Tier 2 items (HVAC, water heater) totaled $11,300. Tier 3 items (cosmetic) totaled $3,000.

They researched the seller. Property listed 52 days. One price reduction. Seller relocated for work and carrying two mortgages. High motivation.

They set three positions: Opening $22,000, Fallback $17,500, Walk-away line (all Tier 1 addressed).

Seller countered at $10,000—testing their resolve. They moved to fallback, emphasized Tier 1 safety issues, referenced seller's timeline pressure.

Final agreement: $18,000 in concessions. All Tier 1 resolved, most Tier 2 covered, Tier 3 dropped. Buyers secured 67% of documented costs because they had a system.

Success: Strategic Thinking Creates Real Outcomes

The buyers who secure the best deals aren't the loudest or most aggressive. They're the most prepared. They know their priorities, their numbers, and their limits before entering the room.

When you follow this framework, three things happen. First, sellers take you seriously because you present data instead of demands. Second, you stay calm under pressure because you've already decided what you'll accept. Third, you walk away from bad deals before they become expensive mistakes.

The property you're negotiating today could be your home for the next ten years. Strategic preparation now protects you from decades of financial regret.

Negotiation isn't about winning. It's about securing a safe, affordable property that aligns with your priorities. Data gives you leverage. Strategy gives you control. Together, they turn information into outcomes.

Now you have a complete negotiation strategy—priorities defined, positions calculated, seller motivation analyzed, and execution timeline mapped. But strategy only works if you can protect it during the most critical window of the buying process: the inspection contingency period. How you use contingency rules, documentation timing, and negotiation sequencing determines whether your strategy translates into real concessions or just wasted preparation.

Chapter 12 Key Takeaways

□ Data without strategy is expensive information—categorize issues into Tier 1, 2, and 3 based on safety and cost

□ Get three contractor quotes for every repair to build negotiation leverage with real numbers, not estimates

□ Analyze seller motivation through days on market, price reductions, and timeline pressure indicators

□ Define three positions before negotiating: opening (ideal), fallback (realistic), and walk-away (non-negotiable)

□ Present evidence packages with inspection excerpts, quotes, and insurance data—not emotional demands

□ Set 48-72 hour response deadlines to maintain negotiation momentum and prevent seller stalling

□ Walk away if Tier 1 safety issues remain unaddressed—no property is worth compromising your security

----

Chapter Resources

Feel free to skip ahead if you'd like to continue reading.

Chapter 13

The Inspection Contingency Playbook

By the time Mia and Jordan won the bidding war, they were tired.

Six offers. Two buyers had waived inspection. Their offer kept a 10-day inspection contingency and still beat the others because they closed fast and were fully approved.

On Day 3, the inspector's report landed in their inbox.

- Roof: near end of life within 3-5 years
- HVAC: past expected age, noisy on startup
- Moisture staining behind the downstairs bath

They did not guess at the cost. Three contractors sent written bids by Day 5. Total documented repairs: $18,900.

That afternoon, their agent sent a calm, clear request:

"Based on the inspection and attached bids, we're requesting an $18,900 credit at closing to address roof, HVAC, and moisture repairs."

The seller's reply on Day 6 was the classic lowball:

"We'll offer $4,000 as a goodwill gesture."

Mia and Jordan did not panic. They did not accept. Their agent replied professionally:

"We understand your position. However, the inspection documented specific issues with repair bids attached. We're requesting the full $18,900, or we'll need to exercise our contingency by the deadline on Day 10."

Your contingency is leverage, not a threat. The deadline makes the seller choose: negotiate or lose the deal.

The seller called on Day 8 with a counteroffer: $13,000. Mia and Jordan accepted. They saved money, protected themselves, and closed on time. The contingency worked because they used it strategically.

Why Most Buyers Waste Their Protection

Most buyers treat inspection contingencies like insurance policies. They assume the protection exists but never plan how to use it. When the inspection reveals real issues, they freeze.

They don't know when to push for full repairs, when to negotiate credits, or when to walk away. The contingency sits unused or gets waived under pressure. Sellers learn quickly which buyers understand leverage and which ones don't.

□ **RED FLAG #1:** You waive the inspection to win the offer without understanding what you're giving up. Inspection contingencies protect your earnest money and give you exit rights. Once waived, you own the home's problems.

The gap isn't information. It's execution. Buyers know inspections matter, but they don't know how to turn findings into negotiation power.

Most buyers fear the contingency will kill the deal. Strategic buyers know it protects their investment.

How Contingency Leverage Works

Your inspection contingency is a deadline-driven negotiation tool. Used correctly, it creates pressure that forces the seller to respond.

Standard inspection periods run 7-17 days depending on your state. During this window, you can request repairs, negotiate credits, or exit the contract with your earnest money returned.

The seller knows three facts:

1. If they refuse repairs, you can walk away
2. If you walk, they restart the listing process
3. Every day that passes reduces their options

This creates natural pressure. The closer you get to the deadline, the more motivated the seller becomes to keep the deal alive.

□ **ACTION STEP 1:** Order your inspection within 48 hours of contract acceptance to maximize your negotiation window.

The Four-Step Leverage Timeline

Day 1-3: Inspection Completion

Schedule immediately. Inspectors book quickly in competitive markets. Waiting until Day 5 leaves no time for contractor bids or specialist follow-ups.

Day 4-6: Contractor Bids

Get written repair estimates for every major issue. Documented costs carry weight. Vague concerns do not.

□ **ACTION STEP 2:** Request written bids from licensed contractors for all major repairs found during inspection. Attach these to your negotiation request.

Day 7-8: Formal Request

Send a clear, professional request listing specific issues with attached contractor bids. Reference your contingency deadline explicitly.

Day 9-10: Deadline Pressure

If the seller stalls or lowballs, remind them of the approaching deadline. This creates urgency without ultimatums.

Strategic buyers use the contingency timeline to build pressure naturally. The deadline does the work for you.

What Makes a Strong Negotiation Request

Your request should include:

- Specific issues from the inspection report
- Written contractor bids for major repairs

- Clear dollar amounts for requested credits or reductions
- Professional tone that references the contingency deadline

Avoid emotional language. Stick to documented facts and repair costs.

Emotion loses negotiations. Documentation wins them.

Warning Signs During Negotiation

Not every inspection issue deserves negotiation. Strategic buyers know when to push and when to walk.

> □ **RED FLAG #2:** The seller refuses to address safety issues like electrical hazards, foundation movement, or structural damage. This signals either financial inability or unwillingness to negotiate. Both are problems.

Watch for sellers who:

- Delay responses until the contingency deadline forces your hand
- Offer token credits far below documented repair costs
- Refuse specialist inspections for major concerns
- Claim "as-is" listing status after accepting your contingency-based offer

These tactics test your resolve. Prepared buyers call the bluff.

> □ **RED FLAG #3:** Your agent pressures you to accept lowball concessions to "keep the deal alive." Remember: your agent gets paid when you close, not when you walk away. Listen to their advice, but make your own decision.

When Walking Away Is Success

Some inspection findings justify immediate exit:

- Major foundation issues requiring engineering reports
- Active mold or water intrusion beyond surface fixes
- Electrical systems creating fire hazards
- Structural damage affecting home safety

□ **ACTION STEP 3:** If inspection reveals major structural, electrical, or safety issues and the seller refuses to address them, exercise your contingency before the deadline.

Walking away protects you from financial disaster. Your earnest money returns. You avoid owning someone else's expensive problem.

Exercising your contingency is not failure. It's protection working exactly as designed.

Your Step-by-Step Execution Plan

Before You Make an Offer

□ **ACTION STEP 4:** Confirm your contract includes inspection contingency language and verify the timeline (typically 7-17 days depending on state).

Know your state's standard contingency period. Understand what "satisfactory to buyer" means legally. Some states require objective findings. Others allow subjective buyer discretion.

During Inspection Period

Day 1-2: Order Inspection

Schedule with a licensed, experienced inspector. Attend if possible. Ask questions. Take photos of concerning items.

□ **ACTION STEP 5:** Attend your inspection and take detailed photos of any issues. Documentation strengthens your negotiation position.

Day 3-5: Get Contractor Bids

For every major issue, request written estimates from licensed contractors. Roofing problems need roofer quotes. HVAC issues need HVAC specialist bids.

Day 6-7: Submit Repair Request

Send a formal request listing specific items with attached bids. Be clear about what you want: repairs completed, credits at closing, or price reduction.

□ **ACTION STEP 6:** Submit your repair request by Day 6-7 of your contingency period with all documentation attached. This gives the seller time to respond before your deadline.

Day 8-10: Negotiate or Exit

The seller will respond with acceptance, counteroffer, or refusal. Evaluate their response against documented costs. If they refuse reasonable requests on major issues, exercise your contingency.

After Seller Response

If they accept your request or make a reasonable counteroffer, proceed to closing. If they refuse or lowball significantly below documented costs, you have two choices:

1. Accept the home as-is if you're willing to cover repair costs yourself

2. Exercise the contingency and protect your earnest money

Never waive your right to walk away before getting the seller's response in writing.

Critical Timing Rules

□ **ACTION STEP 7:** If exercising your contingency, notify the seller in writing before your deadline expires. Late notices forfeit your earnest money protection.

Missing the contingency deadline by even hours can cost you thousands in forfeited earnest money. Calendar the exact date and time. Submit written notice before the clock runs out.

□ **RED FLAG #4:** You verbally tell your agent you're exercising the contingency but don't submit written notice before the deadline. Verbal communication doesn't count. Written notice protects your earnest money.

Matching Strategy to Your Budget

Your inspection contingency strategy depends on how much repair cost you can absorb.

Conservative Approach: Request full documented repairs for any issue over $1,000. Walk away if seller refuses to address major problems.

Moderate Approach: Focus negotiation on items over $5,000. Accept responsibility for minor repairs under $2,000.

Aggressive Approach: Only negotiate safety issues and major systems. Accept cosmetic and minor maintenance items as buyer responsibility.

Match your approach to your financial capacity and comfort with home repairs.

There's no "right" tolerance level. The right strategy is the one aligned with your budget and risk comfort. A $5,000 roof repair might be acceptable to one buyer and a dealbreaker to another.

Some buyers budget for repairs upfront, expecting to negotiate credits later. Others need every system working before closing. Both approaches work when executed with clear documentation and deadline awareness.

Your contingency protects your choice—whether that choice is negotiating hard or walking away.

Real Results From Strategic Use

CASE STUDY: The Strategic Negotiation Win

A couple found $18,900 in documented repairs during inspection. The seller initially offered only $4,000. Instead of accepting or walking away, they:

- Submitted contractor bids with repair breakdowns
- Referenced their contingency deadline professionally
- Noted they had backup properties ready

The seller accepted a $13,000 credit—69% of documented costs, well above typical concession amounts. Strategic contingency use turned pressure into negotiation power.

CASE STUDY: The Clean Exit

Another buyer discovered major foundation movement during inspection. Engineering quotes came back at $42,000, far beyond their budget. The seller refused to address safety items, insisting the home was sold as-is.

The buyer exercised the inspection contingency on Day 9. Their $8,000 earnest money was returned within a week. They immediately moved to a backup property and closed three weeks later.

By walking away, they avoided $42,000 in future costs and protected their family from long-term safety issues. Exercising the contingency was not a setback—it was success.

Using your contingency well leads to one of two positive outcomes:

1. Strong negotiation wins when the seller collaborates
2. Clean protection when the seller refuses reasonable repairs

Both outcomes save money, reduce stress, and put you in control.

The contingency doesn't guarantee repairs. It guarantees choice. That's more valuable.

Chapter 13 Key Takeaways

□ Inspection contingencies are deadline-driven negotiation tools, not insurance policies

□ Document all major issues with written contractor bids before submitting repair requests

□ Submit repair requests by Day 6-7 of your contingency period to maximize pressure

□ The closer you get to the deadline, the more motivated sellers become to negotiate

□ Walking away from major safety or structural issues is success, not failure

□ Never waive contingency rights before getting seller responses in writing

□ Written contingency notice before deadline protects your earnest money

□ Match your negotiation strategy to your financial capacity and repair comfort level

Now you've reached an agreement with the seller. They're offering concessions—but how should you receive them? A price reduction and a repair credit are not the same.

Chapter 14 reveals the strategy behind PRICE REDUCTION VS. REPAIR CREDITS—and how this choice shapes your payment, equity, and long-term costs for the next 30 years.

Chapter Resources

Feel free to skip ahead if you'd like to continue reading.

Contingency leverage starts before inspection. The most effective inspection negotiations begin with property intelligence you already have—flood zones, environmental concerns, fire risk, climate projections—before the inspector even arrives. Generate pre-inspection reports at **HomeDataReports.com** that reveal risks inspectors won't research. Our risk calculator shows you what to expect from specialized inspections before you order them. Create your free account and get your first Essential report covering risks beyond the inspection scope.

Install the Chrome extension to research properties before scheduling showings. Share this with your home inspector—when inspectors join our partner network, they can review property intelligence before arriving onsite, improving assessment focus and efficiency. The digital toolkit includes inspection contingency templates and contractor bid organizers. The video masterclass shows buyers using pre-inspection data to strengthen contingency negotiations. The audiobook reinforces timing frameworks while you're coordinating inspections. Inspection contingencies work best when backed by comprehensive data, not just the inspector's findings.

Chapter 14

Price Reduction vs. Repair Credits

Jack and Melissa found their perfect home—$400,000, great schools, solid neighborhood. Then the inspection report arrived: $25,000 in repairs. Foundation cracks. Roof issues. HVAC on its last legs.

Their agent gave them three options. Price reduction. Repair credit. Or have the seller fix everything before closing.

Jack wanted the price reduced. Lower the sale price, shrink the loan, pay less interest over 30 years. Simple math.

Melissa wanted the credit. They only had $8,000 in savings after the down payment. They needed cash at closing to handle the repairs without going broke in month one.

Their agent wanted the seller to fix it. Clean close, move-in ready, no contractor headaches.

All three options cost the seller $25,000. But they don't all cost the buyer the same.

This is the most overlooked decision in home buying. The structure matters as much as the number. And most buyers choose based on gut feeling instead of actual financial analysis.

The structure of your concession determines your 30-year costs—not just your closing costs.

Why This Decision Matters More Than You Think

When sellers agree to $25,000 in concessions, they don't care how it's structured. Their net proceeds are identical whether they drop the price, write a check at closing, or hire contractors.

But for you? The choice impacts everything.

Price reduction lowers your monthly payment and saves thousands in interest over the life of the loan. But it requires you to have cash reserves to handle repairs after closing.

Repair credits put money in your pocket at closing when you need it most. But they don't reduce your loan amount, so you're paying interest on that $25,000 for the next 30 years.

Seller completion means you move into a repaired home with no contractor management required. But you lose control over quality, timing, and often wind up with the cheapest fixes the seller can negotiate.

And here's where it gets worse: **lender limits restrict how much can be structured as a credit.**

Conventional loans cap seller credits at 3-9% of the purchase price depending on your down payment. FHA loans allow up to 6%. VA loans permit 4%. If your $25,000 in repairs requires a 6% credit on a $400,000 home, you're capped at $24,000. The rest must come out of your pocket or restructured as a price reduction.

Most buyers don't know these limits exist until they're deep into the transaction. Then they scramble to restructure the deal—often losing negotiating leverage in the process.

> □ **RED FLAG #1: Credit Limits** Lenders cap repair credits at 3-9% of purchase price. A $30,000 credit on a $350,000 home with 5% down exceeds the 3% conventional limit. Verify your loan type's maximum BEFORE negotiating structure.

How Each Structure Actually Works

Let's run the real numbers on Jack and Melissa's situation. $400,000 purchase price. $80,000 down payment (20%). $320,000 loan. Current interest rate: 6.25% for a 30-year fixed mortgage.

Option 1: $25,000 Price Reduction

New purchase price: $375,000. New loan amount: $295,000.

Monthly payment drops from $1,970 to $1,816. That's $154/month in savings.

Over 30 years, that's **$55,440 in payment savings**. But the actual benefit is even larger—you're avoiding **$15,500 in interest charges** on the $25,000 that's no longer part of your loan.

Total 30-year benefit: approximately **$18,000 in pure interest savings** (after accounting for the time value of money).

The trade-off: You need $25,000 in cash reserves after closing to handle the repairs yourself.

Option 2: $25,000 Repair Credit

Purchase price stays at $400,000. Loan stays at $320,000. Monthly payment stays at $1,970.

You receive $25,000 at closing to fund repairs immediately.

The trade-off: Over 30 years, you'll pay approximately **$23,000 in interest** on that $25,000 because it's embedded in your mortgage at 6.25%.

Net cost compared to price reduction: **$18,000-$20,000 more** in total payments over the loan's life.

But if you don't have $25,000 in reserves, this structure keeps you from financial disaster in months 1-6 of homeownership.

□ **ACTION STEP 1:** Calculate your post-closing cash reserves. Subtract down payment, closing costs, and 3 months of expenses from available funds. If the result is less than required repair costs, repair credits are your only viable option.

Option 3: Seller Completes Repairs

Purchase price stays at $400,000. Loan stays at $320,000. No cash changes hands at closing.

The seller hires contractors, manages the work, and provides proof of completion before you close.

Best case: Repairs are done properly, you move into a fixed home, and you keep your cash reserves intact.

Worst case: Seller hires the cheapest contractors, work is rushed, final walkthrough reveals shoddy repairs, and you're forced to either accept it or kill the deal after 45 days of wasted time.

Seller-completed repairs transfer financial risk but eliminate quality control.

Price reductions save $15,000-$20,000 over 30 years but require cash reserves. Repair credits provide immediate liquidity but cost $18,000-$23,000 in long-term interest. Seller completion removes your repair burden but introduces quality and timeline risk.

Warning Signs to Watch For

Price Reduction Red Flags

Appraisal risk increases when you reduce the price. If the home was already appraising at contract price, a $25,000 reduction might trigger lender questions about why the value dropped mid-transaction.

If your appraisal comes in low, the price reduction becomes your only option—but now you've lost negotiating power because the seller knows you need it.

> ◻ **RED FLAG #2: Appraisal Timing** Never negotiate price reductions before the appraisal is complete. If the home appraises low, you've already given away your leverage. If it appraises at contract price, you maintain full negotiating power for structure choice.

Repair Credit Red Flags

Lender credit limits vary by loan type and down payment amount. Exceeding them kills the deal structure entirely.

FHA loans cap credits at 6% of purchase price. VA loans allow 4%. Conventional loans range from 3% (less than 10% down) to 9% (25%+ down).

On a $350,000 home with 5% down, your conventional loan caps credits at $10,500. If you need $15,000 in repairs, you'll either pay $4,500 out of pocket or restructure as a hybrid (partial credit, partial reduction).

Seller Completion Red Flags

Timeline delays are common. Contractors run late, materials backorder, weather interferes. Your rate lock expires in 45 days. If repairs aren't done, you either extend your lock (costing $500-$1,500) or walk away.

Quality control is zero. The seller's contractor has one goal: pass the final inspection for minimum cost. You discover poor workmanship six months later when the "fixed" roof starts leaking again.

□ **RED FLAG #3: Contractor Accountability** Seller-hired contractors have no relationship with you post-closing. Include re-inspection clauses requiring licensed inspector sign-off on all completed work. Standard "seller completes repairs" language provides no quality protection.

□ **ACTION STEP 2:** Request a detailed cost breakdown for all seller-completed repairs. Compare pricing against 2-3 independent contractor quotes you obtain. Overpriced estimates indicate lowest-bidder work.

How to Structure Your Request

Don't present one option and hope the seller accepts. Present three options simultaneously and let the seller choose. This increases acceptance rates and eliminates back-and-forth negotiations.

Structure your request as three choices:

Option A (Best for Buyer): $25,000 price reduction **Option B (Balanced):** $15,000 price reduction + $10,000 repair credit **Option C (Best for Seller):** $25,000 repair credit

All three options cost the seller exactly $25,000. But they let the seller pick the structure that fits their situation best—increasing the likelihood they say yes to one of them.

If the seller needs to close fast, they'll pick Option A (price reduction) because it requires no contractor coordination.

If the seller already hired contractors or has relationships with repair vendors, they might accept seller completion.

If the seller is cash-tight at closing, they'll prefer Option C (credits) because it preserves their net proceeds until closing day.

□ **ACTION STEP 3:** Submit repair requests within 24 hours of inspection completion. Delayed requests signal weak negotiating position. Include three structure options in initial submission—don't wait for seller counters.

Offering structure choice increases acceptance rates by 20-40% compared to single-option demands.

Matching Structure to Your Financial Situation

Your structure choice depends on three factors: liquidity, monthly budget constraints, and long-term cost tolerance.

High liquidity buyers (strong cash reserves post-closing) should always prioritize price reductions. The $15,000-$20,000 in interest savings over 30 years outweighs the inconvenience of managing repairs after closing.

Low liquidity buyers (minimal reserves after down payment and closing costs) require repair credits regardless of long-term costs. Running out of cash in month three because you couldn't afford emergency repairs costs far more than $20,000 in interest over 30 years.

Monthly budget-constrained buyers benefit from price reductions even with moderate liquidity. Lowering the monthly payment by $150-$200 creates breathing room for unexpected expenses and reduces default risk.

□ **ACTION STEP 4:** Calculate your break-even point. Divide total interest cost difference by monthly payment savings. If it exceeds 10 years and you plan to sell within 7 years, repair credits may cost less than projected.

CASE STUDY: Hybrid Structure Optimization

Sarah and Tom negotiated $25,000 in concessions on a $385,000 home. They had $12,000 in post-closing reserves—not enough for all repairs, but too much to justify pure credit structure.

They structured it as: **$17,000 price reduction + $8,000 repair credit**

Results:

- Monthly payment dropped $115 (from $2,165 to $2,050)
- Long-term interest savings: $18,000
- Immediate cash for urgent repairs: $8,000
- Total optimization: Both monthly budget relief AND reduced lifetime costs

If they'd taken all $25,000 as credit, they'd have paid $18,000-$20,000 more over 30 years with zero monthly payment benefit.

Monthly payment reduction and cash at closing cannot both be optimized simultaneously—choose based on your weakest financial position.

The Results: What Proper Structure Delivers

Jack and Melissa faced that exact choice. $25,000 in repairs. Limited savings. Tight monthly budget.

A pure price reduction would have required them to fund all repairs from their $8,000 in remaining cash reserves—leaving them with zero emergency buffer. A pure repair credit would have cost them $18,000-$20,000 in interest over 30 years and provided no monthly payment relief.

They chose the hybrid: **$17,000 price reduction + $8,000 repair credit.**

Monthly payment dropped from $2,165 to $2,050—saving $115/month and nearly $18,000 in lifetime interest charges. The $8,000 credit funded the most critical repairs immediately. Total concessions: $25,000, fully optimized for both short-term cash flow and long-term costs.

This is the transformation the Home Data system creates.

You began with property intelligence. You turned risk into documented costs. You learned strategic negotiation. And now you've optimized every dollar you earned in concessions.

You now have The Property Risk Playbook—every tool, every tactic, every template to negotiate with complete confidence.

This system does not guarantee the perfect home. It guarantees you will never overpay, never accept unnecessary risk, and never walk into a purchase unprepared.

The Home Data system delivers information advantage—not just for one decision, but for every decision across the entire transaction.

□ **ACTION STEP 5:** Before submitting your offer, download the complete negotiation template at HomeDataReports.com/playbook. It includes structure options, lender limit charts, and hybrid optimization calculators.

Chapter 14 Key Takeaways

□ Price reductions save $15,000-$20,000 over 30 years but require cash reserves to fund repairs post-closing

□ Repair credits provide immediate liquidity but cost $18,000-$23,000 in long-term interest charges

□ Lender credit limits (3-9% of purchase price) restrict maximum allowable credits based on loan type and down payment

□ Seller-completed repairs eliminate your contractor management but remove quality control and timeline certainty

□ Presenting three structure options simultaneously increases acceptance rates by 20-40%

□ Hybrid structures (partial reduction + partial credit) optimize both monthly cash flow and lifetime costs

□ Structure choice should match your financial position: liquidity level, monthly budget constraints, and long-term planning horizon

----

Chapter Resources
Feel free to skip ahead if you'd like to continue reading.

Financial decisions require accurate data. Calculating whether price reductions or repair credits save you more money depends on understanding total cost of ownership—including insurance premiums driven by property risk. Visit **HomeDataReports.com** to generate reports showing flood insurance costs, fire coverage availability, earthquake premiums, and climate-related expense projections. Our risk calculator reveals ongoing costs that affect break-even analysis between price structures. Create your account and receive your first Essential report free—including insurance cost estimates that factor into your 30-year calculations.

Download the Chrome extension to research risk-driven costs while evaluating properties. Tell your lender and financial advisor about our partner program—when they join our referral network, they can access property intelligence that improves financial guidance for clients. The digital toolkit includes price reduction vs. credit calculators with insurance cost integration. The video masterclass shows real examples of buyers choosing optimal concession structures using comprehensive cost data. Make financial decisions based on complete information, not partial assumptions.

Chapter 15

Final Thoughts

You made it!

By now, you understand something most homebuyers never figure out: **negotiation isn't about being aggressive. It's about being informed.**

It's not about making threats or playing hardball or hoping the seller "feels bad" for you. It's about documentation, timing, leverage, and understanding how the game actually works.

And now you know how the game works.

What You've Learned:

Over the last several chapters, you've built a complete negotiation framework.

You learned **why most buyers negotiate from weakness**—because they don't understand what sellers actually fear, what creates pressure, or how to build leverage from documented facts instead of emotional appeals.

You learned **how to use inspection contingencies strategically**—not as insurance policies you hope you never need, but as deadline-driven negotiation tools that create real pressure when used correctly.

You learned **the difference between price reductions and repair credits**—and more importantly, you learned how to calculate which one saves you more money over 5, 10, or 30 years based on your specific loan terms and ownership timeline.

You learned **when walking away is success**—how to recognize bad-faith sellers, protect your earnest money, and exercise your contingency rights before deadlines expire.

Most importantly, you learned **how to think like a strategic buyer instead of an emotional one.**

That's not a small shift. That's the difference between closing deals you regret and closing deals you're confident about for decades.

You're Not Afraid Anymore:

Here's what I hope changed while reading this book:

You're not intimidated by inspection reports anymore. You know how to read them, how to get contractor bids, how to document findings, and how to turn pages of technical jargon into clear negotiation requests.

You're not confused about contract language anymore. You know what contingencies protect you, when deadlines matter, and how to exercise your rights without forfeiting earnest money.

You're not paralyzed by seller counteroffers anymore. You know how to evaluate whether a response is reasonable, when to push back, and when to walk away cleanly.

You're not guessing about financial structures anymore. You can calculate break-even points, compare long-term costs, and choose the concession structure that actually saves you money instead of just sounding good.

You understand your leverage. And that changes everything.

Sellers can't lowball you and hope you accept out of fear. Agents can't pressure you into bad deals because you "don't want to lose the house." Inspectors can't overwhelm you with findings because you know how to prioritize, document, and negotiate.

You're operating from strength now. Not because you're tougher or more aggressive than other buyers—but because you're **more informed.**

What Happens Next:

Close this book. Take a breath. And then go put this knowledge to work.

When you start researching properties, you'll already know what data to pull. (If you read Book 1, you know how to access federal databases for flood zones, environmental risks, climate projections, and seismic data. If you haven't read it yet, that's your next step—because negotiation strategy works best when built on solid property intelligence.)

When you make an offer, you'll structure it with contingencies that protect you, not weaken you.

When your inspection report arrives, you'll already know the process: document the issues, get contractor bids within 48 hours, submit your request by Day 6-7 with professional formatting and clear deadline references.

When the seller responds, you'll evaluate their counteroffer against your documented costs, your budget, and your walk-away threshold—not against your emotional attachment to the property.

And when you close, you'll do it with **complete clarity** about what you negotiated, what you saved, and what risks you accepted with full awareness.

That's the goal. That's what this book exists to create.

The Resources You'll Need:

This book taught you the strategy. Now you need the data and the tools.

For comprehensive property intelligence: Visit **HomeDataReports.com** to generate detailed risk assessment reports that aggregate federal data from FEMA, NOAA, USGS, EPA, Census, and other authoritative sources. These reports give you the foundation—the documented risks, the environmental context, the climate projections—that you'll use to negotiate from strength.

We're working toward helping tens of thousands of property buyers every month across the United States through HomeDataReports.com and our affiliated websites. The platform exists because buyers deserve access to the same data professionals use—without spending weeks learning how to interpret federal databases.

For the full education: If you haven't read **Book 1** yet, that's where you learn how to research property risk using federal data sources. Book 2 assumes you have that knowledge and teaches you how to **use it strategically during negotiations.** Together, they create the complete system.

For what's coming next: This is just the beginning. We're building additional books covering advanced topics like investment property analysis, multi-family negotiation strategies, and long-term portfolio building. We're creating video courses that walk you through real transaction examples step-by-step. We're developing tools, templates, and calculators that make the tactical work faster.

The goal isn't just to help you buy **one** house successfully. The goal is to give you frameworks that work for every real estate decision you make over the next 30 years—purchases, refinances, sales, investment properties, helping family members, evaluating market conditions.

Real estate knowledge compounds. The more you understand, the better every future decision becomes.

One Last Thing:

Most homebuyers will never read this book.

They'll make offers based on emotion. They'll waive contingencies because everyone else is doing it. They'll discover problems during inspection and have no idea how to convert findings into leverage. They'll accept whatever the seller offers because they don't know what's reasonable or how to push back professionally.

They'll close on properties having left thousands—sometimes tens of thousands—of dollars on the table.

You're not going to be one of those buyers.

You know too much now. You understand the process. You've seen the frameworks. You know what creates leverage, how timing works, when to negotiate and when to walk.

All that's left is execution.

So go execute.

Find the property that makes sense for your life, your budget, and your long-term goals. Pull the data. Run the numbers. Make a strategic offer with proper contingencies. Use your inspection period intelligently. Document everything. Negotiate from strength. Protect your earnest money if things go sideways.

And close with confidence—not anxiety.

That's the difference this book makes. That's what strategic knowledge creates.

You've got the tools. You understand the game. You're ready.

Now go get the terms you deserve.

— Damian Martinez
Founder, HomeDataReports.com

Continue your education:
Book 1: Property risk assessment using federal data sources
HomeDataReports.com: Comprehensive property intelligence reports
Future releases: Advanced courses, tools, and resources for strategic buyers
You're not negotiating alone anymore. You're negotiating informed.

Chapter Resources
Feel free to skip ahead if you'd like to continue reading.

Your negotiation journey continues beyond this book. Everything you've learned becomes more powerful when backed by comprehensive property intelligence. Visit **HomeDataReports.com** to create your free account and access the data foundation that makes strategic negotiation possible. Test our proprietary risk calculator on properties you're considering. Download your first Essential report free—covering flood, fire, seismic, environmental, and climate risks in one clear document. Install our Chrome extension for instant property research while browsing real estate sites.

Share this platform with everyone in your circle—friends, family, realtors, lenders, insurance agents, home inspectors, contractors. Professionals who join our partner referral network can provide property intelligence to their clients, building stronger relationships through better information. Explore the audiobook for reinforcement while commuting. Invest in the digital toolkit for templates, calculators, and checklists. Take the video masterclass for real transaction examples and advanced strategies. This isn't just about buying one house—it's about building knowledge that compounds across every real estate decision for the next 30 years.

Chapter 16

Appendix: Essential Resources and Reference Guide

This appendix provides quick access to key federal data sources, legal references, and practical tools mentioned throughout the book. For detailed case studies and strategic frameworks, refer to the relevant chapters.

Federal Property Risk Data Sources

These government databases provide the foundational data for property risk assessment:

FEMA Flood Maps and Risk Data

- URL: msc.fema.gov
- Provides flood zone designations, historical flood claims, and community participation in National Flood Insurance Program
- Free access to all U.S. properties

NOAA Climate Data

- URL: ncdc.noaa.gov
- Historical weather patterns, storm frequency, temperature trends
- Essential for understanding long-term climate risks

USGS Earthquake and Geological Data

- URL: earthquake.usgs.gov

- Seismic activity records, fault line mapping, soil composition data
- Critical for properties in seismically active regions

EPA Environmental Data

- URL: epa.gov/enviro
- Superfund sites, air quality, water contamination, radon zones
- Environmental hazard screening for any U.S. address

U.S. Census Bureau

- URL: data.census.gov
- Population trends, economic indicators, demographic shifts
- Context for neighborhood stability and growth patterns

National Weather Service Storm Data

- URL: weather.gov
- Tornado, hurricane, severe storm records by location
- Historical context for extreme weather exposure

> All six federal databases are publicly accessible at no cost. They provide the same data used by professional risk assessment services, but require interpretation and cross-referencing to generate actionable insights.

Key Legal Cases and Disclosure Requirements

Johnson v. Davis (Florida, 1985) Established that sellers must disclose material defects affecting property value, even if not directly asked. Landmark case defining seller disclosure obligations.

Easton v. Strassburger (California, 1984) Required real estate agents to conduct visual property inspections and disclose observable defects. Expanded agent liability for known property issues.

Strawn v. Canuso (New Jersey, 1995) Held that builders must disclose off-site environmental hazards (nearby landfill) affecting property desirability. Extended disclosure requirements beyond property boundaries.

State Disclosure Requirements Overview

Most states require seller disclosure forms covering:

- Known structural defects
- Major system failures (roof, HVAC, plumbing, electrical)
- Environmental hazards (lead paint, asbestos, mold, radon)
- Flood zone designation
- Homeowner association rules and fees
- Material facts affecting value or desirability

Disclosure standards vary significantly by state. California, Illinois, and New York require comprehensive written disclosures. Texas, Florida, and Pennsylvania have standardized disclosure forms. Some states rely primarily on common law principles rather than statutory requirements.

> □ **RED FLAG:** Seller disclosure forms ask "Are you aware of..." rather than "Does the property have..." This creates incentive for willful ignorance. Sellers who avoid inspections can legally claim they weren't aware of issues.

Insurance and Risk Assessment Resources

National Flood Insurance Program (NFIP)

- URL: floodsmart.gov
- Official flood insurance quotes and zone verification
- Required for mortgaged properties in high-risk flood zones

Insurance Information Institute

- URL: iii.org
- Consumer guides on homeowners insurance, natural disaster coverage
- State-by-state insurance requirements and average costs

Reinsurance Association of America

- Publishes catastrophe loss data and risk modeling information
- Industry perspective on geographic risk pricing

State Insurance Departments Citizens Property Insurance (Florida), FAIR Plans (California), and state-backed insurers of last resort provide coverage when private insurers withdraw from high-risk markets. Contact your state insurance department for availability and pricing.

Appraisal and Valuation Standards

The Uniform Standards of Professional Appraisal Practice (USPAP) governs licensed appraiser conduct. Key principles affecting homebuyers:

- Appraisers must use comparable sales from the past 6-12 months
- Adjustments for differences between subject property and comparables must be documented and reasonable
- Appraisers cannot have financial interest in transaction outcome
- Market conditions (seller concessions, days on market) must be considered

When challenging an appraisal, provide recent comparable sales data the appraiser may have missed, documentation of property improvements not reflected in the report, or evidence of errors in property description or adjustment calculations.

Price Reduction vs. Repair Credit Quick Reference

Price Reduction Benefits:

- Reduces loan amount and total interest paid
- Increases immediate equity
- Lowers property tax basis in most jurisdictions
- Decreases down payment requirement (percentage-based)
- Better for buyers planning to refinance or sell within 5-7 years

Repair Credit Benefits:

- Preserves appraisal value for minimum down payment requirements

- Allows buyer to choose contractors and quality of repairs
- Tax-deductible in year paid (for investment properties)
- Easier for seller to accept (doesn't reduce list price)
- Better for buyers planning long-term ownership (10+ years)

Break-Even Analysis: For loans under 4.5% interest, price reductions typically save money within 5-7 years due to reduced interest payments. For loans above 6% interest, price reductions create immediate and sustained savings. Repair credits make sense when appraisal value matters more than long-term interest costs.

State-Specific Considerations

California: 17-day inspection contingency standard. Sellers must complete Transfer Disclosure Statement and Natural Hazard Disclosure.

Texas: 7-10 day inspection periods common. Sellers complete Seller's Disclosure Notice. No mandatory home inspection requirement.

Florida: 10-15 day inspection periods typical. Sellers complete Seller's Property Disclosure Statement. Hurricane and flood risk disclosures required in coastal areas.

New York: "As-is" sales more common. Attorney review of contracts standard. Property Condition Disclosure Act requires seller disclosure form for residential properties.

Pennsylvania: Seller Property Disclosure Statement required. 10-day inspection period typical. Buyers have legal right to hire licensed inspectors.

States with highest disclosure requirements: California, Illinois, Maine, New York, Oregon, Rhode Island, Washington.

States allowing "as-is" sales with minimal disclosure: Alabama, Arkansas, Georgia, Missouri, North Carolina, South Carolina, Virginia.

Quick Action Checklist

Before Making an Offer:

- Review property disclosure forms for red flags
- Research flood zone designation and insurance costs
- Check local crime statistics and school ratings
- Verify property taxes and HOA fees

- Confirm inspection contingency included in contract

During Inspection Period:

- Schedule inspection within 48 hours of contract acceptance
- Attend inspection and document issues with photos
- Get written contractor bids for all major repairs
- Submit repair request by Day 6-7 with documentation
- Exercise contingency before deadline if seller refuses reasonable repairs

Negotiating Concessions:

- Calculate break-even point for price reduction vs. credit
- Verify lender allows requested credit amount
- Get seller agreement in writing before deadline
- Confirm appraisal supports requested changes
- Document all repair completion requirements

Before Closing:

- Verify all agreed repairs completed with permits
- Review closing disclosure 3 days before closing
- Confirm final loan terms match agreed structure
- Check for last-minute seller concession limits
- Schedule final walkthrough 24 hours before closing

The federal data is free. The legal framework is established. The negotiation strategies are proven. What separates successful buyers from frustrated ones is execution—using available tools at the right time with proper documentation.

Additional Resources

Book-Specific Tools: Visit HomeDataReports.com/playbook for downloadable worksheets, calculators, and templates referenced throughout the chapters.

Continuing Education: Property risk assessment, real estate law, and market conditions evolve. Follow updates from FEMA, EPA, and state insurance departments for changes affecting property values and insurance availability in your area.

Professional Guidance: This book provides strategic frameworks for informed decision-making. For specific legal questions, consult a licensed real estate attorney. For complex financial calculations, work with a qualified mortgage professional or CPA.

About the Development of This Book

Modern Book Development Process

This book was created using AI-assisted writing tools to accelerate the drafting process and improve the organization and clarity of complex concepts. The workflow combined human expertise with AI capabilities:

Author Role:

Designed all chapter structures, analytical frameworks, and strategic methodologies

Provided source data, concepts, and direction for each section

Selected, modified, and approved all AI-generated content

Conducted fact-checking against federal databases and market research

Made final editorial decisions on all material included in the book

AI Tool Role:

Assisted with drafting text based on author-provided concepts and structures

Improved explanation clarity for technical topics

Enhanced organizational flow and readability

Accelerated conversion of ideas into structured written content

What AI Did NOT Do:

Originate the core risk analysis frameworks or negotiation strategies

Provide professional opinions or advice about specific properties

Make recommendations about transactions, contracts, or real estate decisions

Replace human judgment, expertise, or fact-checking

The resulting content reflects the author's perspectives, experience, and interpretation of publicly available federal data and real estate market dynamics. AI tools served as drafting assistants, not content creators or professional advisors.

Continued Disclaimer

As stated in the legal disclaimer at the beginning of this book, this material is provided solely for educational and informational purposes. It does not constitute legal, real estate, insurance, tax, engineering, or financial advice. Readers must consult licensed professionals before making any property-related decisions and remain fully responsible for their own choices and outcomes.

END OF APPENDIX

This appendix is designed as a quick reference guide, not an exhaustive academic resource. For detailed case studies, strategic frameworks, and step-by-step instructions, refer to the relevant chapters throughout the book.

Chapter Resources

Feel free to skip ahead if you'd like to continue reading.

Chapter 17

Glossary of Terms

This glossary defines key real estate negotiation and transaction terms used throughout this book. Terms are listed alphabetically for easy reference.

As-Is Condition

A property sale where the seller makes no repairs and provides no warranties about condition. Buyers accept the property in its current state, though inspection contingencies may still allow buyers to walk away if issues are discovered.

Appraisal

An independent professional evaluation of a property's market value, typically required by lenders before approving mortgages. Low appraisals can affect negotiated price reductions and repair credits.

Appraisal Contingency

A contract clause allowing buyers to cancel or renegotiate if the property appraises for less than the purchase price. Protects buyers from overpaying based on appraiser's independent valuation.

Base Flood Elevation (BFE)

The calculated elevation of floodwater during a 100-year flood event. Properties below BFE typically require flood insurance and may face higher premiums.

Break-Even Point

The timeframe when cumulative savings from one financial structure (e.g., price reduction) equals another (e.g., repair credit). Used to determine optimal concession strategies based on ownership timeline.

Closing Costs

Fees and expenses paid at closing, including title insurance, appraisal fees, recording fees, and lender charges. Seller concessions can offset these costs.

Closing Disclosure

A standardized document providing final loan terms and closing costs, delivered at least 3 business days before closing. Shows all negotiated credits and price adjustments.

Comparative Market Analysis (CMA)

A report comparing the subject property to recently sold similar properties, used to determine fair market value and assess negotiation leverage.

Contingency

A condition in a purchase contract that must be satisfied for the contract to remain binding. Common contingencies include inspection, appraisal, and financing. Protects buyer's earnest money if conditions aren't met.

Contingency Deadline

The date by which a contingency must be satisfied or waived. Missing deadlines can forfeit earnest money and eliminate buyer's right to cancel.

Contingency Exercise

The formal act of invoking a contingency right to cancel a contract or renegotiate terms. Requires written notice delivered before deadline expiration.

Contractor Bid

A written estimate from a licensed contractor detailing repair scope, materials, labor costs, and timeline. Essential documentation for repair request negotiations.

Days on Market (DOM)

The number of days a property has been actively listed for sale. Extended DOM often signals negotiation opportunity or underlying property issues.

Due Diligence

The buyer's process of investigating a property before closing, including inspections, title review, insurance quotes, and risk assessment.

Earnest Money Deposit (EMD)

Money deposited by the buyer to demonstrate serious intent to purchase. Held in escrow and applied to closing costs or down payment. Forfeited if buyer cancels without valid contingency.

Escrow

A neutral third-party account holding earnest money deposits, down payments, and closing funds until transaction completion. Also refers to the closing process itself in some states.

FHA Loan

Federal Housing Administration-insured mortgage with lower down payment requirements (3.5%) but stricter property condition standards and seller concession limits (typically 6%).

Inspection Contingency

A contract clause allowing buyers to conduct property inspections and negotiate repairs or cancel the contract based on findings. Expires after a specified period (typically 7-17 days).

Inspection Period

The timeframe during which buyers can conduct inspections and submit repair requests. Begins at contract acceptance and ends at contingency deadline.

Letter of Intent (LOI)

A preliminary non-binding agreement outlining proposed purchase terms before formal contract. Rare in residential transactions but common in commercial deals.

Licensed Contractor

A construction professional authorized by state or local government to perform specific types of work. Required for repair bids used in professional negotiations.

Listing Agreement

The contract between seller and listing agent establishing commission, listing price, marketing terms, and duration. Affects seller motivation and negotiation flexibility.

Loan-to-Value Ratio (LTV)

The percentage of a property's value financed through a mortgage. Higher LTV limits seller concessions and affects pricing negotiation strategies. Example: $180,000 loan on $200,000 property = 90% LTV.

Multiple Listing Service (MLS)

A database of properties for sale, accessible to licensed real estate agents. Provides comparable sales data, days on market, and listing history.

Offer

A formal written proposal to purchase property at specified terms, including price, contingencies, closing date, and requested concessions.

Permit

Government authorization required for specific construction, renovation, or repair work. Unpermitted work can affect value, financing, and negotiation leverage.

PMI (Private Mortgage Insurance)

Insurance required by lenders when down payments are less than 20%. Price reductions can reduce PMI costs by lowering loan amounts.

Price Reduction

A negotiated decrease in the purchase price. Reduces loan principal, total interest paid, property tax basis, and down payment requirements. Alternative to repair credits.

Purchase Agreement

The legally binding contract between buyer and seller outlining all transaction terms, including price, contingencies, closing date, and included items.

Repair Credit

Money provided by the seller at closing for buyer-completed repairs. Preserves appraisal value but increases loan amount and long-term interest costs. Alternative to price reductions.

Repair Request

Formal written communication from buyer to seller requesting specific repairs or concessions based on inspection findings. Should include contractor bids and reference contingency deadlines.

Satisfactory to Buyer

Contract language giving buyers sole discretion to determine whether inspection results or property condition meets their standards. Broad protection for buyers in many states.

Seller Concession

Money or credits provided by the seller to offset buyer's closing costs, repairs, or other expenses. Subject to lender limits based on loan type and LTV ratio.

Seller Concession Limits

Maximum percentage of purchase price that sellers can contribute toward buyer's costs, set by loan program. Examples: Conventional 3% down = 3% limit; FHA = 6%; VA = 4%.

Seller Disclosure

Required form where sellers reveal known property defects, repairs, insurance claims, and other material facts. Varies significantly by state.

Title

Legal ownership of real property. Title insurance protects against ownership disputes, liens, and other claims against the property.

Title Contingency

Contract clause allowing buyers to cancel if title issues (liens, easements, ownership disputes) cannot be resolved before closing.

Unpermitted Work

Construction, renovation, or repairs completed without required government permits. Can affect financing, insurance, and create negotiation leverage for buyers.

VA Loan

U.S. Department of Veterans Affairs-guaranteed mortgage available to eligible veterans and service members. Requires properties to meet specific condition standards with 4% seller concession limits.

Walk-Through (Final)

Buyer's inspection of the property 24-48 hours before closing to verify agreed repairs were completed and property condition hasn't changed since contract signing.

Written Notice

Formal documentation required for exercising contingencies, submitting repair requests, or communicating contract-related decisions. Verbal communications typically don't satisfy legal requirements.

Zoning

Government regulations controlling how property can be used (residential, commercial, agricultural). Zoning violations can create negotiation leverage and affect property value.

Connect with Damian:
Website: HomeDataReports.com
Location: South Florida
Mission: Empowering homebuyers through data-driven decision-making
Other Books by Damian Martinez:

The Home Data Handbook - Book 1: Property Risk Assessment (Standard & Expanded Editions)

Future releases covering advanced investment strategies, portfolio building, and specialized market analysis

Additional Resources:

Comprehensive property intelligence reports at HomeDataReports.com

Free Chrome extension for instant property research

Video masterclass and digital toolkit for strategic buyers

Audiobook editions for learning on the go

Damian Martinez wrote this book because he believes the American Dream deserves a foundation built on truth, not surprises.

Chapter 18

About the Author

Damian Martinez is the founder of HomeDataReports.com, a platform dedicated to helping homebuyers make informed, data-driven decisions using comprehensive property intelligence reports.

After working as a licensed real estate agent from 2017 to 2019, Damian witnessed first-hand the critical gaps in the homebuying process—buyers making six-figure decisions with incomplete information, discovering costly surprises after closing, and relying on outdated disclosure systems that failed to protect their interests.

Frustrated by an industry that prioritized transactions over transparency, Damian left traditional real estate to build something better: a system that aggregates federal data from FEMA, NOAA, USGS, EPA, the U.S. Census Bureau, and other authoritative sources into actionable property intelligence reports accessible to every buyer, not just industry insiders.

In 2020, Damian purchased his own home using the exact methodology outlined in this book—checking flood maps, evaluating seismic risks, reviewing environmental data, and calculating long-term cost-of-ownership scenarios before making an offer. That experience validated what he already knew: informed buyers make better decisions.

Since founding HomeDataReports.com, Damian has helped tens of thousands of property buyers across the United States understand the risks associated with their potential purchases—not to discourage homeownership, but to empower buyers with the information they need to negotiate better, avoid preventable surprises, and choose properties that align with their goals and risk tolerance.

Damian's work is driven by a simple philosophy: every home has risks, but every buyer deserves to understand those risks before signing a contract. Property intelligence shouldn't be a luxury reserved for sophisticated investors or industry professionals—it should be accessible, understandable, and actionable for everyone.

When he's not analyzing property data or building new tools for homebuyers, Damian can be found in South Florida, refining the systems and strategies that help buyers across the country make smarter real estate decisions.

Learn more and access property intelligence tools at: HomeDataReports.com

Chapter 19

Your Next Step: Turn Knowledge Into Action

You've finished the book. Now it's time to put what you've learned to work.

Visit **HomeDataReports.com** and create your free account today. Here's what you get immediate access to:

Your First Essential Report - FREE

Generate a comprehensive property intelligence report for any U.S. address at no cost. See exactly what federal data reveals about flood zones, wildfire risk, earthquake hazards, environmental concerns, and climate projections.

Proprietary Risk Calculator

Test our advanced risk assessment tool on unlimited properties. Get instant risk scores across multiple categories before making offers or scheduling showings.

Free Chrome Extension

Install our browser extension and research properties in real-time while browsing Zillow, Realtor.com, or Redfin. One click pulls comprehensive risk data without leaving the listing page.

Partner Referral Network

Are you a realtor, lender, insurance agent, home inspector, or contractor? Join our partner network and provide professional-grade property intelligence to your clients. Build stronger relationships through better information.

Additional Resources

Digital Toolkit: Templates, calculators, checklists, and documentation guides

Video Masterclass: Real transaction examples with step-by-step walkthroughs

Audiobook Edition: Reinforce frameworks while commuting or researching properties

Future Releases: Advanced courses, investment strategies, and specialized market analysis

Share With Your Network

Know someone buying a home? Share HomeDataReports.com with friends, family, and colleagues. Help them make informed decisions backed by comprehensive data.

The Bottom Line

This book gave you the frameworks. The platform gives you the data.

Knowledge without execution is just theory. Data without strategy is just numbers.

You now have both.

Visit **HomeDataReports.com** today.

Create your account. Run your first report. Download the Chrome extension.

Start making real estate decisions the way informed buyers do—with complete awareness, strategic confidence, and authoritative data.

The American Dream deserves a foundation built on truth, not surprises.

HomeDataReports.com

Comprehensive property intelligence for every U.S. address.

Ready to Put This Knowledge to Work? Scan to access:

- Your FREE property risk report
- The audiobook edition
- The digital toolkit
- The video masterclass
- And more resources for confident homebuyers at homedatareports.com/books

Made in United States
North Haven, CT
04 November 2026

21767237R00099